973.7 STE
Stein, R. Conrad.
Escaping slavery on the Underground
Railroad
DEC 26 2008

DATE DUE			

FROM MANY CULTURES,
One HISTORY

ESCAPING SLAVERY ON THE UNDERGROUND RAILROAD

R. Conrad Stein

Enslow Publishers, Inc.
40 Industrial Road
Box 398
Berkeley Heights, NJ 07922
USA
http://www.enslow.com

Library of Congress Cataloging-in-Publication Data

Stein, R. Conrad.
   Escaping slavery on the Underground Railroad / R. Conrad Stein.
     p. cm. — (From many cultures, one history)
   Includes bibliographical references and index.
   ISBN-13: 978-0-7660-2799-2
   ISBN-10: 0-7660-2799-6
   1. Underground Railroad—Juvenile literature. 2. Fugitive slaves—United
     States—History—19th century—Juvenile literature. 3. Antislavery
     movements—United States—History—19th century—Juvenile literature.
     4. Abolitionists—United States—History—19th century—Juvenile literature.
     5. Slavery—United States—History—Juvenile literature. I. Title.
   E450.S825 2008
   973.7'115—dc22
                            2007015124
Printed in the United States of America

10 9 8 7 6 5 4 3 2 1

To Our Readers: We have done our best to make sure all Internet Addresses in
this book were active and appropriate when we went to press. However, the author
and the publisher have no control over and assume no liability for the material
available on those Internet sites or on other Web sites they may link to. Any
comments or suggestions can be sent by e-mail to comments@enslow.com or to the
address on the back cover.

Every effort has been made to locate all copyright holders of material used in this
book. If any errors or omissions have occurred, corrections will be made in future
editions of this book.

Illustration Credits: The Connecticut Historical Society Museum, p. 48; Courtesy
of Paul Collins, p. 95; Enslow Publishers, Inc., p. 52; Getty Images, p. 99; The
Granger Collection, New York, pp. 33, 70, 81, 106, 108, 113 (left); Hulton Archive/
Getty Images, p. 12; Levi Coffin House Association and Jane Sharp Holman, pp. 66,
68; Library of Congress, pp. 7, 16, 17, 31, 35, 41, 55, 59, 64, 76, 85, 90, 103, 111, 112,
113 (right); Mary Evans Picture Library/The Image Works, pp. 37, 77; Photo by
Mark Bealer Photography, courtesy of the National Underground Railroad Freedom
Center, p. 107; Shutterstock.com, p. 22.

Flag Illustration Used in Book Design: ©2007 Jupiterimages Corporation

Cover Illustration: © Private Collection, Peter Newark American Pictures/The
Bridgeman Art Library

Contents

CHAPTER One

Escape of Tice Davids

Tice Davids ran for his life. He was an escaped slave who had just broken away from his owner's farm in northern Kentucky. Davids sought only the freedom that many other people enjoyed. But in the eyes of the law, he was a criminal. By the act of escape, he had stolen his owner's "property." Now his owner pursued him through the woods and the fields. Davids heard the dogs barking behind him. His owner carried a shotgun. Davids's life could end at any moment.

Davids ran wildly as thorns from bushes tore his clothing and scratched his skin. Gasping for breath, he climbed a hill. At the top he saw what he deemed to be a miracle—the broad Ohio River flowed majestically. This river had been Davids's quest since his escape. Fellow slaves had whispered to him that on the far side of the Ohio were black and white people who hated slavery. Those people would help him gain freedom. Davids raced down the riverbank and plunged into the icy waters.

The owner saw his slave's head bobbing above the river waters. Keeping an eye on the bobbing head, he found a boat and rowed across. He held a shotgun on his lap. The owner reasoned he would force Davids to return to the Kentucky farm. Later, he would punish the slave for the attempted escape.

Davids reached shore at the riverside town of Ripley, Ohio. Finally, luck smiled on him. The town of Ripley was a center of antislavery sentiment. As Davids ran through the streets, he saw a huge white man beckoning him. Once more, Davids was fortunate. The man was a minister named John Rankin. He owned a house high on a hilltop where he kept watch over the riverbank. Rankin considered it his God-given duty to come to the aid of runaways swimming the Ohio. Over the years, Rankin and his sons had helped many slaves escape to freedom. Rankin pointed to a place near a house where Davids could hide.

The slave owner walked the streets of Ripley. Clearly the man was confused. Moments earlier he saw Davids pull himself from the river at this town. Now the slave was nowhere to be found. The owner scratched his head and was heard to say, "[He] must have gone off on an underground road."[1] At the time,

Runaway slaves like Tice Davids often had to navigate, or hide in, rough terrain.

railroads were being developed and were capturing the American imagination. Also at the time, a network of people dedicated to helping escaped slaves was being formed. Thus, a legend was born. The "underground road" that frustrated the Kentucky slave owner began to be called the "Underground Railroad."

Is the Tice Davids escape true or is it a story? It is known that a slave named Tice Davids swam to freedom in 1831. There was nothing new to this escape. Hundreds of slaves fled from their owners every year. Many fugitive slaves were assisted on their flight by Americans who believed that slavery was both immoral and sinful. Beginning in the early 1830s, this group of people fighting slavery came to be called the Underground Railroad. Perhaps the Tice Davids story helped to create the legendary name.

The Underground Railroad was not a railroad, nor did it run underground. Instead, it was a fellowship of men and women who risked their lives to help slaves escape their bondage. By necessity, the Underground Railroad was a loosely organized institution. Its members were lawbreakers. People who assisted runaway slaves could be sent to prison or suffer even worse punishments. Members of the Underground Railroad knew only a few other members. They used railroad terms when discussing their activities. Runaways were called "passengers."

Those who assisted the passengers were "conductors." Houses where escapees could rest were "stations." Owners of the stations were "stationmasters."

Because no records were kept, it is not known how many men and women served on the Underground Railroad. Nor is it known how many slaves the Railroad helped escape.

The Underground Railroad is a heroic chapter in American history. Its membership consisted of black and white men and women. The organization helped to destroy the nation's greatest evil—slavery. Tales of the Underground Railroad and the dangers faced by Railroad workers and escapees have been told for generations. Still, those tales remain fresh and alive. Stories of courage never age.

CHAPTER Two

A Firebell in the Night

"Slavery enriches not the mind, heart, or soil where it abides; it curses and blights everything it comes in contact with it. Away, away with [it], tear up by the roots these noxious weeds which choke the growth of all fair plants, and sow in their stead the beautiful flowers of freedom."[1]

—Peter Randolph (1825–1897),
an ex-slave from Virginia

Slavery in the Land of the Free

"We hold these truths to be self evident, that all men are created equal," read the bold words of the United States Declaration of Independence. Yet, at the time those words were written, slavery was practiced in every one of the Thirteen Colonies that would become states. Thomas Jefferson was the primary author of the Declaration of Independence. Yet, Jefferson himself owned many slaves.

Today, Americans hail their country as a beacon of freedom and the hope of the world. More than two hundred years ago, American men and women made the same boast. They claimed the United States was the freest place on Earth. How could a people practicing slavery dare to call themselves free? The reasons behind this contradiction lie deep in United States history.

A Slow Beginning

In 1619, a Dutch ship approached the struggling English settlement at Jamestown, Virginia. The ship put ashore twenty Africans in exchange for goods needed to complete the trip.[2] Technically, the newcomers were not slaves. Laws of the colony did not recognize slavery as an institution. The Africans were classified in Jamestown record books as indentured servants. Such servants customarily worked unpaid for a period of time (usually seven years) and then they were free to make their own livings. However, there is no record of these twenty Africans making indentured-servitude contracts with the Dutch.

In the late 1600s, attitudes toward Africans began to change. Greed no doubt contributed to the shift in thinking. English indentured servants were citizens of England, and had the right to eventual

This engraving shows the arrival of a Dutch ship with a group of Africans at Jamestown, Virginia, in 1619.

freedom. Africans were citizens of no recognized country. They had no such rights. The practice of slavery elsewhere was also taken into account by English colonists. Thousands of African slaves toiled on plantations in the nearby Spanish colonies of Cuba and Mexico. The slaves of the Spaniards were not given freedom after a time of servitude. Finally, racism entered the white mind-set. Blacks were thought of as lesser human beings than whites. They

Blacks in the New World

Certainly the Africans who settled at Jamestown in 1619 were not the first blacks in the Americas. Historians believe at least one crewmember of Christopher Columbus' ship, which crossed the Atlantic in 1492, was black. Blacks also accompanied some of the Spanish explorers that came to the New World after Columbus. Black slaves were then brought to the Caribbean region and to South America.

did not come from Christian backgrounds. In the minds of many colonists, the sons and daughters of Africa simply did not deserve freedom.

Africans continued to arrive on the shores of the Thirteen Colonies. By 1641, blacks were classified as slaves. In the early 1700s, enslaved blacks outnumbered whites almost two to one in the Carolina colony.[3] In other colonies, especially to the South, the slave population increased. A census taken in 1720 reported that black slaves outnumbered free whites in every territory south of Maryland.[4]

The growing number of slaves frightened white colonists. Whites sensed bitterness and hatred brewing in the hearts of the slaves. In 1741, a series of mysterious fires swept New York City. Rumors spread that black slaves and poor whites had conspired to burn the city down. To discourage future uprisings, white leaders determined the rebels had to be brutally punished. Hundreds of people were arrested. After hasty trials, thirteen blacks were tied to stakes and burned alive, and eighteen blacks and four whites were hanged.[5]

The American Revolutionary War (1775–1783) shook the practice of slavery. About five thousand blacks (freemen and slaves) fought for the cause of American independence.[6] Some slaves were granted their freedom in return for wartime service. Others took advantage of the confusion bred by warfare and slipped away from their masters. Black soldiers in the colonial army performed well and made an impression on their enemy. A Hessian officer in service to the British reported, ". . . no [American] regiment is to be seen in which there are not Negroes in abundance: and among them are able-bodied, strong, and brave fellows."[7]

The end of the Revolutionary War established the United States as an independent nation. But above the music and fireworks of the victory celebrations, the issue of slavery hung like a dark cloud. Many Americans wanted to ignore the obvious contradiction that slaves lived in their "free" society. Others could not push the hypocrisy out of their thoughts. In 1774, Abigail Adams, the wife of the second U.S. president, wrote to her husband, "It always appeared a most iniquitous scheme to me to fight ourselves for what we are daily robbing

Presidents as Slaveholders

George Washington was America's first president. Washington, who was from Virginia, owned many slaves. Thomas Jefferson, who wrote the Declaration of Independence and was the third president of the United States, also owned slaves. In all, eight of the first twelve American presidents owned slaves at one time in their lives.[8]

and plundering from those who have as good a right to freedom as we have."[9]

King Cotton and the New South

Shortly after the Revolutionary War, slavery began to die out in the northern states with small-scale farms. Immigrants from Europe came to the northern towns and cities. The European newcomers were willing to work for low wages and were seen as future citizens. By 1804, all of the northern states had passed laws to end slavery, New York state being the exception until 1822. It seemed that slavery would come to a gradual end in the South too. But the old system was kept alive largely by a certain crop and a new invention.

Eli Whitney was a skilled mechanic who tinkered with inventions. As a young man, he traveled from his home state of Massachusetts to Georgia to accept a teaching job. While in Georgia, he watched slaves

George Washington (in black) is shown with some of his slaves, who are harvesting grain in this painting.

picking seeds from raw cotton fiber. This process, called cleaning the cotton, was painfully slow. Whitney believed a machine could clean the cotton faster and easier than the manual method. In 1793, Whitney displayed a machine that he had built in only a few days. His invention—the cotton gin—was a remarkably simple device. It fed cotton through a series of comb-like teeth that was turned by a hand crank. The teeth swept the seeds out of the cotton fiber ten times faster than the old method. Larger

Slaves are depicted using a cotton gin in this wood engraving originally published on December 18, 1869.

cotton gins, driven by waterwheels, soon appeared and revolutionized the cotton industry.

Cotton required a long, sunny growing season with little or no frost. These conditions were met especially in the Deep South—Alabama, Georgia, Mississippi, and Louisiana. Soon farmers in those states switched from rice and tobacco to cultivating fields of cotton. In 1790, before the invention of the cotton gin, the South produced only three thousand bales of raw cotton each year. By 1810, the annual production rose to 178,000 bales.[10] Fabulous sums of money were made from this crop which Americans called "King Cotton."

The cotton industry started the great divide in the United States. The North developed as a land of small farmers and business owners. In the South, the people who owned the great plantations wielded enormous political and economic power. Cotton gave the South a society of sharp contrasts. A few wealthy slave-owning planters lived with the comforts and authority of Old World kings and queens. The vast majority of southerners—white and black—struggled to make a meager living.

King Cotton depended on slavery. Raising cotton required hundreds of slaves working on the plantations under a broiling sun. Sugar, which was a major crop in Louisiana, also used large numbers of slave workers. To meet the demand, many slaves were sold from their old homes in Virginia and the Carolinas to the cotton-producing states of Alabama and Mississippi. The price of slaves soared. A man measured his wealth not by the amount of land he owned (as was true in the past) but by the number of slaves he held.

Life of a Slave

Austin Steward was born a slave in Virginia. He began his working life at age eight, helping to clean the kitchen in his master's house. Years later he described his owner, Captain Helm: "Capt. Helm was not a very hard master, but generally was kind and pleasant." However Mrs. Helm, who ran the kitchen where Austin worked, was a brute. "[She] frequently punish[ed] the young slaves herself . . . whipping them with a cowhide, which she always kept by her side when sitting in her room . . . Mrs. Helm appeared to be uneasy unless some of the servants were under the lash."[11]

Reports of cruel treatment abound in slave journals and diaries. Slaves were whipped, clubbed, burned, and tied up in painful positions. Even the "kindly" masters often resorted to the whip to discipline a slave. Austin Steward saw his own mother beaten by Captain Helm with a horsewhip. "[He] whipped my poor mother most unmercifully—far more severely than I ever saw him whip a horse."[12]

Not all slaves were treated in an inhumane manner. Conditions varied greatly from farm to farm and from owner to owner. But always the dealings with an owner followed the slave throughout his or her life. As one ex-slave said, "[There] was not so much brutality in slavery as one might expect . . . the real injury was the making of a human being [into] an animal without hope . . . I know slavery's curse was not pain of the body, but the pain of the soul."[13]

The workday on southern farms started before sunrise. Women and men worked together weeding and raking the soil. The slaves were given short breaks for breakfast and for lunch. Usually they worked until dark. The work shift was extended on nights when a full moon hung in the sky and illuminated the fields. On larger farms, field bosses supervised gangs of twenty or more slaves. Some bosses were black slaves who were given special privileges by the white owners. Often the bosses, called drivers, carried whips with them to punish on the spot any field hand whose work did not meet standards.

Geography ruled much of a slave's fortunes. Life was especially hard for a slave in the cotton-growing areas of the Deep South. A slave in Alabama or Mississippi could not easily break away from the owner. In the Deep South, slaveholders could rule in a cruel manner. Owners had to relax their rules in border states such as Tennessee and Kentucky because escape to the North was much easier. A master knew that an angry slave was more likely to escape. In border regions, the free states to the north lay just one hundred or so miles away. On an Alabama plantation, the land of freedom could be more than one thousand miles distance.

Most slaves lived on farms far from the cities. The few who did live in or near cities enjoyed greater comforts and freedoms than did the rural dwellers. A city-dwelling slave could steal away from the owner and blend in with a community of free blacks.

Price of Slaves

Beginning in 1808, a federal law banned the importation of slaves from Africa or the Caribbean region into the United States. The law was often violated, but it did limit the number of slaves available. The federal law plus the demands for workers in the sugar and cotton fields of the Deep South caused the price of slaves to soar. In 1808, a fieldhand who was young and able-bodied cost $600 in New Orleans slave markets; by 1853 that price had risen to $1,250.[14]

In rural areas, slaves had to have a note signed by their owner in order to merely walk the roads.

Many slaves learned skills such as carpentry, blacksmithing, and bricklaying. Skilled slaves were hired out by owners to work on projects at neighboring farms. In such cases, the owner collected the bulk of the skilled workers' wages. However, a slave could earn money beyond what his owner was paid for his services. If the slave carefully saved extra earnings, he could buy freedom for himself or his family members. This process of buying one's freedom grew more difficult as the price for slaves rose.

Slaves who were employed as house servants fared better than field workers. House servants ate a varied diet and wore more substantial clothes.

Skilled cooks became favorites with the masters' families. Slave women, employed in houses, tended to white babies and watched over the older children. Only the master determined who would work where.

On typical farms, slaves lived in cabins no larger than a modern one-car garage. Families of ten people or more were jammed into one cabin. Slave quarters were drafty and often did not have furniture. Most slaves slept on a dirt floor over a bit of straw. Food for slaves consisted mainly of cornmeal and boiled pork. Because of crowded conditions and

Some slave cabins looked like the modern replica above. Others, however, were in much worse condition than this.

a poor diet, many slaves died of diseases such as cholera and tuberculosis. The diseases struck children first. Slave children who survived the sicknesses were infested with worms and had rotten teeth. Rare was the slave who lived to the age of sixty.

As terrible as conditions were on most farms, a slave lived in constant fear of being sold. Selling meant a person had to leave sisters, brothers, mothers, fathers, and lifelong friends. Slaves could be sold for any reason, very often simply because the owner needed money. Slaves were "property" and were often given as gifts. Owners realized the slaves' fear of being sold, and regularly threatened them with sale if their work became substandard. Slaves in the upper South used the term being sold "down-river" as their ultimate tragedy. Downriver meant the sugar or cotton plantations farther south along the Mississippi.

The development of the cotton industry caused a massive shift of slaves from the upper South to the lower South. Owners in Virginia and Maryland, who had kept the same slaves for generations, now sold them to plantations in the Deep South in order to take advantage of the high prices. The misery felt by the uprooted slaves cannot be measured or even imagined today. They were marched, often chained together, hundreds of miles to their new destinations. Some fell into a deep depression and refused to eat during the march. Suicides were frequent. Other transported slaves developed mental illness while trekking south.

Emily Russell was a young woman facing the ordeal of being sold. Born in Virginia, she was known as one of the prettiest young ladies in the region. The man interested in buying her owned a house of prostitution in New Orleans. Emily's mother had bought her own freedom and worked as a washerwoman in New York City. The mother saved her pennies with the intention of freeing all her children. In desperation, Emily wrote her mother, "My dear mother will you please come [to get me] as soon as you can? I expect to go away very shortly. Come now and see your distressed . . . daughter once more."[15] Emily's owner wanted eighteen hundred dollars as a purchase price for her. The mother could not raise that much money. In 1850, Emily Russell was sold to the man from New Orleans. She died on the trip south. Fellow slaves said she died of a broken heart.

Intelligent whites who were churchgoers and proud to call themselves Christian still defended slavery. They said they were "civilizing" the blacks by introducing them to Christianity. Genteel whites called their workers servants, not slaves. They claimed they treated the slaves as if they were members of their own family—and often this was the case. But even the genteel slaveholders had to close their hearts to the fundamental argument that all people yearn to be free and to command their own destiny.

Thomas Jefferson was the third president of the United States. Born in Virginia, he was a slaveholder all his life. Still, he hated the institution of slavery. Jefferson believed slavery disgraced and degraded the owner as well as the slave. Moreover, he felt the practice of slavery brought grave dangers and tensions to his countrymen. Year by year, slavery edged the nation toward a separation between North and South and a possible civil war. In a famous letter written near his death, Jefferson said slavery alarmed Americans, frightening them, ". . . like a firebell [ringing] in the night."[16]

CHAPTER Three

Striking Back at Slavery

"[**Y**ou] take the Bible as your standard of Christian duty. But sir, know ye not that in the light of this book, you have been acting the hypocrite all this while!"[1]

> —*The runaway slave Henry Bibb, writing to his former owner from his home in Canada in 1852*

Resistance and Rebellion

Enslaved men and women found unique and sometimes ingenious ways to fight the system that controlled their lives. On occasion, all of the slaves on a farm agreed to a secret work slowdown in order to punish an unfair owner. To the owner's despair, the people stopped working as soon as the overseer's back was turned. Mysterious events plagued farms when slaves entered into silent agreements to frustrate the work schedule. Tools were broken or went missing. Fires broke out in sheds and barns. The exasperated owner could blame no individual slave for these mishaps. A reasonably intelligent owner was able to recognize the work of a slave conspiracy. The owner then had to treat his people with at least a degree of respect if he wanted the farmwork to continue.

Individual slaves resisted their owner through a practice called absconding or lying out. When lying out, a slave literally took to the woods and hid there for a period of time. Fellow slaves sent food to the runaway's hideout. Often an owner was forced to negotiate with an absconding slave. The owner sent a fellow slave to the woods to talk to the fugitive. In many cases the owner agreed not to punish a slave if he or she returned. A Missouri slave named Delcia Patterson absconded when she was transferred from the house staff to work in the fields. Her owner sent word that if she returned she could continue her duties in the house. She came back and later said, "No one ever bothered me anymore, either."[2]

Though they were slaves, the African Americans struggled to build their own inner freedoms. Through religion, music, and family devotion, the enslaved people gained some control over their own lives.

Religion was the joy as well as the salvation for slaves. Slaveholders commonly pronounced Sundays as a day of rest. They encouraged everyone to attend Sunday church services. At first, most large plantations had at least one black preacher. Beginning in the 1830s, however, rumblings of black revolt were being felt in white society. Slaveholders feared the black preachers were passing along hidden messages of rebellion in their sermons. So, plantation owners paid white preachers to conduct services. Sermons delivered by whites stressed obedience to the slave owners and the promise of a wonderful life after death.

Often a secret black church meeting was conducted on Sunday afternoons. These meetings took place after the approved church services concluded. In the secret services, black preachers delivered a different sermon to the congregation. They told the story of Moses who led the Hebrew people out of slavery. They spoke of Jesus, a slave to no man. The Bible, as taught by black ministers, gave the slaves hope. Music brought relief and happiness to the slave community. Work songs helped weary men and women endure their fourteen-hour shifts in the fields. Despite the dismal lives led by the slaves, much of their music was bright and lively. Some songs taken up by the slaves remained popular for a long time:

> *When I was young I used to wait*
> *On Master and give him his plate,*
> *And pass the bottle when he got dry,*
> *And brush away the blue tail fly.*

Chorus

Jimmy crack corn and I don't care,
Jimmy crack corn and I don't care,
Jimmy crack corn and I don't care,
My master's gone away.[3]

Not surprisingly, there is a note of sadness in much of slave music. Like most folk songs, the slave ballads told a story. A lullaby called "All the Pretty Little Horses" tells of a slave woman whose job it was to tend a white baby. Lovingly she holds the infant in her arms and sings to him. But the woman's thoughts are on her own baby who is lying unattended in a dank slave cabin. She refers to her own child in the chorus.

Hush-a-bye, don't you cry,
Go to sleep-y, little baby.
When you wake, you shall have cake,
And all the pretty little horses.
Blacks and bays, dapple grays,
Coach and six white horses.
Hush-a-bye, don't you cry,
Go to sleep-y, little baby.

Chorus

Way down yonder in the meadow,
There's a poor little lambie;
The bees and butterflies pickin' out his eyes.
The poor thing cries, "Mammy."[4]

Slaves found their greatest strength through devotion to their families. Strong attachments

Calling the Tune

Some slaveholders exercised such strict control over their crews that they even dictated what work songs they could sing. An 1851 advice book called *Management of Negroes* told owners; "While at work [the songs] should be brisk. I have no objection to their whistling or singing some lively tune, but no drawling tunes are allowed in the field, for their [work] motions are certain to keep time with the music."[5]

developed to close family members as well as to aunts, uncles, and cousins. Most owners permitted slave men and women to hold their own wedding ceremonies. In the eyes of the slaves, marriage vows were binding. However, the law did not recognize slave marriages. An owner could break up a family by selling a wife, a husband, a mother, or a child. A slave named Hannah Chapman remembered when her father was sold off to a neighboring plantation. "That was a sad time for us." The father often sneaked away at night to visit his family. Chapman said, "When his Master missed him he would beat him all the way home. [We] could track him the next day by the blood stains."[6]

Slave Uprisings

Denmark Vesey was an ex-slave black carpenter who lived in Charleston, South Carolina. In 1822, rumors

Stories of the slave uprising in St. Domingue, today known as Haiti, frightened slave owners in the United States. This engraving shows black rebels hanging French soldiers.

swirled that Vesey was planing to lead a slave revolt. Blacks far outnumbered whites in the Charleston region. If a black rebellion broke out, the bloodletting would be horrible. Probably Vesey was planning such a massive assault. White authorities learned of the plans. Hundreds of blacks were arrested and punished. Denmark Vesey was hanged.

Denmark Vesey had heard about events in the Caribbean island of St. Domingue. In 1791, the slaves of St. Domingue revolted against their French masters. A former slave named Toussaint L'Ouverture led the Haitian slaves. Scores of whites were killed in the uprising. The victorious slaves renamed the nation Haiti, which is a near neighbor with the southern United States. Whites fleeing Haiti landed on southern shores, especially around New Orleans. They told horror stories about the savagery unleashed during a slave revolution. The stories added fuel to white fears.

Nat Turner was born a slave in 1800 in Virginia. Whenever he had the opportunity, Turner walked in the woods to think and be alone. A deeply religious man, he developed a vision. He believed he was destined to become a savior, such as Moses or Jesus, and lead his people to freedom. In 1831, the slaves of Southampton County, Virginia, rose up under Nat Turner. For two days they went on a rampage, killing fifty-nine whites.[7] Finally, Nat Turner was captured

The *Amistad* Mutiny

In 1839 a Spanish ship called *La Amistad* carried about fifty-three African slaves from one Cuban port to another. The slaves revolted, killed several crewmembers, and demanded the captain steer the ship to their homeland in Africa. However, the American navy captured the vessel and took it to New London, Connecticut. A court trial began to determine whether the slaves were murderers or freedom fighters. Seventy-three-year-old John Quincy Adams argued for the slaves. Adams had been president of the United States from 1825 to 1829. The ex-president won the case and the slaves were set free. They elected to return to Africa. In 1997, a popular movie, *Amistad*, told the story of the famous slave mutiny.

African slaves, led by Joseph Cinque, kill Captain Ramon Ferrer during the June 1839 insurrection on board the Spanish slave ship *La Amistad* off the coast of Cuba.

and hanged. Furious whites killed many other blacks, the guilty as well as the innocent.

The possibility of slave rebellions filled white society with terror. Acting on these fears, southern leaders tightened laws regulating slaves. All over the South, white militias were hastily organized and patrolled the countryside. The militias deemed that controlling blacks was their major mission. A slave named Harriet Jacobs remembered:

> [When] Nat Turner's insurrection broke out, the news threw our town into great commotion . . . It was a grand opportunity for the low whites, who had no negroes of their own to scourge [whip] . . . Everywhere men, women, and children were whipped till blood stood in puddles at their feet.[8]

John Brown was a white man who believed God regarded the United States as an evil nation because of its practice of slavery. As Brown aged, he saw himself as a soldier of God who was given divine orders to eradicate slavery from the land.

On October 16, 1859, Brown and a small band of followers seized an arsenal at Harpers Ferry, Virginia. Brown hoped to capture the rifles in the arsenal, issue them to escaped slaves, and begin a holy war.

Brown's holy war never got started. After a battle with the U.S. Army, he was arrested, tried, and hanged. Many Americans in the North hailed Brown as a martyr and a saint. To Southerners he was a dangerous criminal.

John Brown was seen as a hero to some and a violent extremist to others.

Brown's raid on Harpers Ferry intensified the hatred brewing between the two sides and hastened the eventual conflict. In the Civil War, which began sixteen months after Brown's execution, Northern soldiers marched to battle singing a song to the tune of the Battle Hymn of the Republic:

John Brown's body lies a-mouldering in the grave,
John Brown's body lies a-mouldering in the grave,
John Brown's body lies a-mouldering in the grave,

His soul's marching on!
Glory, Halle-Hallelujah!
Glory, Halle-Hallelujah!
Glory, Halle-Hallelujah!
His soul's marching on![9]

The Abolitionists

In 1837, a white man named Elijah Parish Lovejoy printed an antislavery newspaper in the town of Alton, Illinois. Most Alton townspeople thought of him as a troublemaker. Several times people broke into his shop and destroyed his printing press. One night, Lovejoy saw a group of men approaching a warehouse where his new press was stored. He and men who were there with him dashed out to stop them. Someone fired a shot. Elijah Parish Lovejoy was killed on a dusty Alton, Illinois, street. The death made Lovejoy a towering figure in the abolitionist movement.

A Classic Abolitionist Book

Harriet Beecher Stowe was born in Connecticut to an antislavery family. Her father, Lyman Beecher, was an abolitionist preacher and a worker on the Underground Railroad.

In 1852, Harriet Beecher Stowe published the novel *Uncle Tom's Cabin*, which became an antislavery classic. The leading character was Uncle Tom, a humble slave. His owner, Simon Legree, was portrayed as cruel and sinister. A hero of the book is Eliza, a slave woman who escapes to freedom while carrying her baby in her arms. The book was read by thousands of Northerners and brought many over to the antislavery side. *Uncle Tom's Cabin* is one of those rare books that helped to change history.

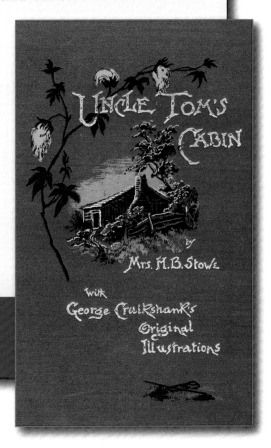

The front cover of Harriet Beecher Stowe's *Uncle Tom's Cabin*.

Abolitionists were men and women who wanted to forbid, or abolish, the practice of slavery. Members of the Quaker church were strong abolitionists. Many women were active in the abolitionist movement. Laws at the time forbade women from voting and limited their ability to own property. Women, deprived of rights themselves, felt a kinship with the slaves. Free blacks also became active members of abolitionist societies.

One of the country's most powerful abolitionists was William Lloyd Garrison. For many years he served as president of the American Antislavery Society. In Boston, he published a newspaper financed by African Americans called *The Liberator*. Several prominent Southerners threatened to kill him. The state of Georgia offered a five thousand-dollar reward for his arrest. Despite these threats, he continued to write bold antislavery statements. In the first issue of *The Liberator* he wrote, "On this subject [slavery] I do not wish to think, to speak, or write with moderation . . . I am in earnest—I will not equivocate—I will not excuse—I will not retreat a single inch—AND I WILL BE HEARD."[10]

Another passionate abolitionist was Frederick Douglass. Born a slave in Maryland, Douglass escaped from his master when he was a young man. In Rochester, New York, he published a newspaper called *The North Star*. A gifted speaker, he traveled in Northern cities giving lectures to antislavery

Reading as a Passage to Freedom

Southern states had laws forbidding anyone from educating a slave. Abolitionist books and pamphlets circulated secretly in the South, and no slaveholder wanted his servants exposed to such literature. But the slaves' desire to read was almost as great as their hunger to be free. Books were smuggled into the slave quarters. In hidden sessions, a slave who managed to master a few written words taught the skill to others.

societies. In his speeches, he publicly declared himself an escaped slave. This meant he could be captured and returned to bondage. At one point he was forced to flee to England to avoid being captured.

Douglass's writing ability and his powerful speaking style led several critics to suggest he was never a slave. Because slaves were not usually taught how to read and write, it is thought he was too well educated and cultured to have spent his youth in bondage. To silence his critics, Douglass published his 1845 autobiography *Narrative of the Life of Frederick Douglass, an American Slave*. The book describes his struggle to learn to read and discover more about the world outside of his slave quarters. He said, "The more I read, the more I was led to abhor and detest my enslavers. I could regard them in no other light than a band of successful robbers . . ."[11]

Passion and excitement ruled abolitionist meetings. In the early 1800s, religious zeal gripped the United States. No abolitionist wanted the sin of slavery to stain his soul in the final meeting with God. Preachers dominated abolitionist meetings. They urged listeners to end slavery now, before they had to face the anger of God in the afterlife. At abolitionist societies, Americans heard women speaking to large audiences for the first time. Even more radical was the fact that blacks stood on the stage and addressed an audience composed of hundreds of whites.

Sojourner Truth was a slave born in New York State. She claimed that as a child she was able to speak with God. The divine conversations led her on the path to being an abolitionist. She became free in 1828 as the result of a New York law banning slavery. Later, she changed her name from Isabella Baumfree (the name given her at birth) to Sojourner Truth. With her deep voice and clever wit, she attracted the attention of hundreds of people at abolitionist meetings. Sojourner Truth often shared the same speaker's platform with Frederick Douglass.

Abolitionists held diverse views about their goals. Some wanted to end slavery immediately. Others worked for the gradual elimination of the slavery system. A large number of Americans favored laws to forbid black slavery in the new states

Sojourner Truth, an abolitionist, was known for her powerful speeches.

opening to the west. Other whites wished to end slavery, yet they believed blacks were inferior. Groups of whites joined colonization movements that aimed to free slaves and then ship them to Africa.

Abolitionists who worked within the Underground Railroad also had wide-ranging beliefs about the goals of their movement. The Railroad was one of America's first integrated organizations. It embraced black and white men and women. Still, it is safe to say all members of the Underground Railroad were abolitionists. They wished to end the practice of slavery immediately.

Railroad members were also lawbreakers who risked jail to aid escaping slaves. The law regarded a slave as property of the owner, and anyone helping that slave achieve freedom was, in the eye of the law, a thief.

In the early 1800s, the nation expanded westward triggering a great debate in Congress: Should slavery laws move west along with the country? Southerners held that the states opening in the West should have laws allowing slavery. Northerners argued the West should be made up of free states, not slave states. Congress tried to pander to both sides by passing a series of compromise laws. The Compromise of 1850 let California enter the Union as a free state, while allowing slavery in Utah and New Mexico if the people of those territories approved. Similar provisions were made in the 1854

Kansas-Nebraska Act. The compromises satisfied no one. In fact, they were stepping stones to war.

For the Underground Railroad, the Compromise of 1850 held special importance. To appease Southerners, Congress attached a new fugitive slave law to the legislation. Fugitive slave laws had existed since the late 1700s. Such laws allowed slaveholders to pursue escapees anywhere in the nation, including the free states. The 1850 law called for severe punishment to anyone assisting an escaped slave.

Another measure that infuriated members of the Underground Railroad was the *Dred Scott* v. *Sandford* decision of 1857. Dred Scott was a slave who lived in Missouri, where slavery was legal. In the 1830s, he traveled with his owner to the free state of Illinois. Scott sued in court. He argued that his residence in a free region should make him free. The case went to the Supreme Court, the highest court in the land. The result was a crushing defeat to Scott and to the antislavery movement. The Court stated that slaves were not U.S. citizens and therefore Scott must remain with his owner. However, the sons of Scott's first owner bought freedom for him and his family in 1857.

To the people of the Underground Railroad, measures such as the Fugitive Slave Law and the *Dred Scott* v. *Sandford* decision were acts to be defied. They heard only God's law—a higher law—which commanded that all men and women must be free.

CHAPTER Four

The Hunted and the Hunters: Early Escapees

"**I** was now about twelve years old, and the thought of being a slave for life [weighed] heavily on my heart."[1]

—Frederick Douglass, from an early chapter in his autobiography

The Hunted

Thousands of slaves escaped their owners before the Underground Railroad was established. The true number who made successful escapes and never returned to bondage is unknown. There was little pattern to the flight of individual slaves. Some planned their breakout for months. They stashed food and spare clothing in cloth bags hidden in the slaves' quarters. Others escaped spontaneously. Many left to avoid being sold. Primarily it was young men, acting alone or in small groups, who made the flight. Women and children did flee, but not as often as men. The young men who dared to escape left loved ones behind. Most harbored plans to buy or spirit away their family members at a later date.

Before 1830, slaves made their breaks for freedom without the help of the Underground Railroad. At that time, the Railroad lacked a firm organization and even a name. Also, the slaves who trekked north were fearful of seeking help from anyone on the way. It was impossible to tell who would prove to be friend or foe.

Jim Pembroke was born a slave in Maryland in 1807. A bright and clever youngster, he learned the blacksmithing trade. As a slave, his work was one of the few joys in his life. Years later he said, "I had aimed to do my work with dispatch and skill, my blacksmith's pride and taste was one thing that reconciled me so long to remain a slave."[2] When he was twenty years old, Pembroke had a conversation with his owner. During their talk, he failed to glance downward as was the custom when a black spoke to a white. Instead, Pembroke made the mistake of looking his owner straight in the eye. For that transgression the owner beat him savagely with a stick.

After the beating, Pembroke decided to run away. In doing so, he was forced to leave his parents, brothers, and sisters behind. Departing from his family saddened him, but he was determined to find a new life as a free man. The farm was in Maryland, not far from the free state of Pennsylvania. Pembroke was only vaguely aware that Pennsylvania was a free state, unlike the slave state where he lived. He could not read, and he had little knowledge of the country in which he lived. Despite his many fears, he stole away from the slave quarters at night. "My only guide was the North Star," he said. "[A]t what point I should strike Pennsylvania, or when or where I should find a friend, I knew not."[3]

Pembroke traveled by night. He knew his master, or men his master hired, would be out on the roads looking for him. If captured, he would certainly be flogged, and then perhaps sold to a plantation in the Deep South. Anyone who spotted him could alert the sheriff that a runaway was on the loose and then collect a reward. Not only was Pembroke friendless, but he also had to view every stranger as a potential enemy. He spent his first day hiding in a cornfield. On his second day, he crouched under a bridge. His only food was a few apples he saw growing on a tree. The apples gave him miserable stomach pains that added to his gloom. The next night, he resumed his journey only to discover he had

The North Star and Freedom

The North Star was a guiding light for runaway slaves. It is believed that blacks who worked as sailors and navigated by the stars taught the slaves to follow the North Star to the free states. The slaves found the North Star by seeking out the Big Dipper and following its handle to find the stationary star that hung in the northern skies. To them, that star glowed as a heavenly beacon. The slaves called the Big Dipper the Drinking Gourd.

been walking south instead of north. He was not only alone and hunted, but he was lost as well.

Finally, Pembroke tried to travel by daylight. He was soon stopped by a group of four white men. One of them was armed with a knife. Laws were written in such broad language that any white person had the right to question a black person and demand to see his or her pass. Pembroke lied. He told the men he was a free black and did not have his freedom papers on his person. No one believed him. The men thought he was a runaway, and they dreamed of collecting a reward. However, the whites got careless. They locked him in the back room of a tavern, and then left to do farmwork. Pembroke managed to slip away.

Once more alone and starving, Pembroke continued his march toward freedom. Clouds covered the night sky, and he could not see the North Star.

Which direction was he going? Where were the free states of the North? It made little difference. He simply wanted to get away—far away. Afraid of walking on the road, he traveled cross-country through forests and farmers' fields. From the darkness, he heard the pounding of horses' hooves and the sounds of men shouting to one another.

Jim Pembroke later changed his name to James W.C. Pennington.

He knew the horsemen were looking for him.

In the morning, Pembroke peered out of the woods and saw the road. He walked carefully along the road, jerking his head around to look behind him every few seconds. At last he saw an elderly white woman. Could he trust her and at least ask where he was? He had to take the chance. He had eaten almost nothing for three days. Finding this lady proved to be a welcome brush with good fortune. "I afterward learned she was a widow, and an excellent Christian woman. I asked her if I was in Pennsylvania."[4] The answer was yes. Next, he asked if there were somewhere he could find work. The woman told him of a Quaker farmer who lived three miles up the road and who would be glad to hire him. "I thanked her and bade her good morning."[5]

Half an hour later, Pembroke knocked on the door of a farmhouse, hoping it was the right place. A white man answered the door. The man smiled at him. Pembroke told the man he was looking for work. "'Well,' said he. 'Come in and take thy breakfast, and get warm, and we'll talk about it . . .'"[6] Pembroke was astonished by the man's trust and generosity. He repeated the words in his mind:

> Come in and take thy breakfast, and get warm. These words spoken by a stranger, but with such an air of simple and fatherly kindness, made an overwhelming impression on my mind. They made me feel, spite of all my fear and timidity, that I had, in the presence of God, found a friend and a home.[7]

Indeed, Pembroke had found a friend. He stayed in the Quaker household for six months. Since he was an excellent worker and a skilled blacksmith, he made himself useful on the farm. Using the Bible, the Quaker farmer and his wife taught Pembroke to read. He never forgot their kindness and their help.

Years later Pembroke wrote a book called *The Fugitive Blacksmith*. In the book, he referred to the farmer only as W.W. The man and his wife broke the law by assisting him, a slave on the run. Pembroke did not want them to get into trouble because of their crime. We now know that "W.W." was William Wright, a man who became a leader of the Pennsylvania Underground Railroad. Pembroke himself changed his name to James W.C. Pennington. He later became a minister. Pennington, too, joined the Underground Railroad and helped slaves flee captivity.

Development of the Railroad

The Underground Railroad, as it was later called, did not exist when James W.C. Pennington ran away. Still, there were people in the South and the North who were willing to help fugitives despite the dangers they faced by doing so. Those quiet, and in most cases, nameless heroes formed the beginnings of what we now hail as the Underground Railroad.

It is generally believed the Underground Railroad got its true beginnings in Pennsylvania and in New Jersey during the early 1800s. At that time, a network of Christians in those states believed it was their duty, given by God, to help escaped slaves. The people hardly knew one another. They simply gave runaways food, allowed them to rest, and directed them to other sympathetic households. In this manner, the escapees reached safe havens in places like Philadelphia, or they traveled as far north as Canada.

In the 1830s, perhaps due to the flight of Tice Davids, the loosely organized group came to be called

Washington's Complaint

Decades before the establishment of the Underground Railroad, some Americans assisted runaway slaves. In 1786, one of George Washington's slaves fled from Virginia and took up hiding in Pennsylvania. In a letter, Washington complained, "it is not easy to apprehend [them] in [Pennsylvania] because there are a great [number of people] there who would rather facilitate their escape . . . than apprehend the runaway."[8]

the Underground Railroad. Its men and women did not want their conversations or their notes to be understood by others. So, the slave helpers used railroad terms as a code. Escapees were passengers. Guides for the escapees were conductors. Safe houses were stations or depots. From 1830 to 1860, the Underground Railroad expanded. Networks were established in Illinois, Indiana, Ohio, Pennsylvania, New York, New Jersey, and the New England states. No records were kept, and much of the railroad's activities are a mystery to this day. What we do know comes from diaries and letters that emerged years after slavery ended. The names of many of the railroad's greatest heroes are lost to history. We do not know exactly how many African Americans fled with the help of the Underground Railroad. Some estimates say the railroad assisted as many as 100,000 fugitives.[9]

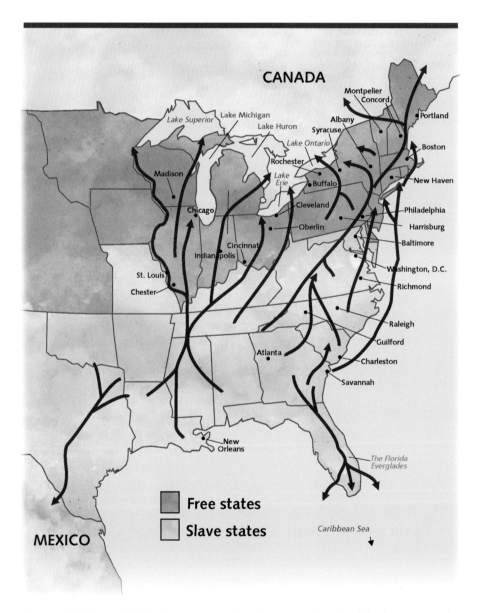

From 1830 to 1860, the network of routes in the Underground Railroad greatly expanded.

The Hunters

The people who pursued runaway slaves had the law on their side. The Fugitive Slave Law of 1850 required sheriffs in the North to apprehend runaways and hold them for their owners. The law also allowed owners or agents of the owners to search anywhere in the nation for escapees. As the number of escapes increased, the slaveholders upped the rewards they were willing to pay. The plight of fugitives in the South as well as the North became more dangerous.

Laws gave rise to legions of what were called slave catchers. Generally, slave catchers were impoverished whites who hunted down fugitives with the aim of collecting a reward. Most did not work for a particular owner. Instead they made pursuits based on the size of the reward an owner was willing to pay. Slave catchers were regarded as vile men. Often they were shunned even by their white neighbors who approved of slavery.

When a slave escaped, the owner sent out word and posted a reward. Slave catchers roamed the vicinity searching for the runaway. Any black could be stopped, questioned, and apprehended. The blacks had no right to a jury trial. Slave catchers regularly captured free blacks and sold them into slavery. There was little blacks could do to fight this system. Laws supported the slave catchers.

The Escape of "Box" Brown

Henry Brown was a slave who worked on a Virginia tobacco farm. He decided to run away after his owner sold his wife and child. Over the years, Brown had befriended a white salesman named Samuel Smith who was from Pennsylvania. Smith dropped hints that he was a member of an antislavery society and would help Brown break free.

Brown developed a plan: "The idea suddenly flashed across my mind of shutting myself up in a box, and getting myself conveyed as dry goods to a free state." Smith approved the plan and sent word to a Philadelphia antislavery office to watch for such a crate. Brown squeezed inside a box that was smaller than a casket. He had a fellow slave nail the lid shut. Air holes were drilled in the box, and a sign was painted on the top: THIS SIDE UP. The crate was put on a train for Philadelphia.

During most of the trip, the box was carelessly turned upside down. Brown was now standing on his head. "I felt my eyes swelling as if they would burst from their sockets." After an hour and a half in this "dreadful position," Henry Brown arrived in Philadelphia and was freed from the box by antislavery workers. Brown made his flight in 1849. In the lore of the Underground Railroad, he is known as Henry "Box" Brown.[10]

Slave catchers frequently used specially trained dogs to track down runaways. Most of the dogs were bloodhounds, famed for their keen senses of smell. With their noses to the ground, the dogs tracked the scent of a fleeing slave. A slave hunter named David Turner who lived in Tennessee advertised his services in a local newspaper: "BLOOD-HOUNDS—I have TWO of the FINEST DOGS for CATCHING NEGROES in the Southwest. They can take the trail TWELVE HOURS after the NEGRO HAS PASSED,

Slave hunters sometimes shot at runaway slaves.

and catch him with ease. I am ready at all times to catch runaway negroes."[11]

Fear of slave uprisings in the South led to a practice called patrolling. Patrollers were low-paid police officers who were hired by local government to guard rural regions and discourage any form of slave misbehavior. The patrollers spread a reign of terror among the slaves. Even a white owner had no right to keep patrollers off his or her property. Patrollers pounded on doors of slave cabins and demanded entrance. A fugitive slave named Lewis Clark told an abolitionist audience, "If a slave don't open his door to them [the patrollers] at any time of night they break it down. They steal his money if they can find it, and act just as they please with his wives and daughters."[12]

John Capeheart was a patroller and a slave catcher in Norfolk, Virginia. He wrote:

> It was part of my business to arrest all slaves and free persons of color, who collected in crowds at night, and lock them up . . . I did this without any warrant, and at my own discretion. Next day they are examined and punished. The punishment is flogging. I am one of the men who flog them. They get not exceeding thirty-nine lashes. I am paid fifty cents for every Negro I flog. The price used to be sixty-two and a half cents. I am paid fifty cents for every Negro I arrest, and fifty cents more if I flog him. I have flogged hundreds. I am often employed by private persons to pursue fugitive slaves. I never refuse a good job of that kind.[13]

The North, an Uncertain Haven

Slaves held in captivity saw the North as a living dream. It was like Canaan, the land promised to the Hebrew people in the Bible. However, this promised land did not always provide a safe haven for the fugitive. The 1850 Fugitive Slave Law allowed owners to pursue runaways in the North as well as the South. Wording in the law said, "all good citizens [are] commanded to aid and assist in the prompt and efficient execution [of the slave's recapture]."[14] Many Northern communities resisted the slaveholders who tracked down fugitives on their soil. But high rewards tempted some Northerners to turn in an escapee. A runaway named William A. Hall had made his trek as far north as Wisconsin. Hall was warned, "[T]here are men here now, even where you are living, who would betray you for a half a dollar if they knew where your master is."[15] Hall fled to Canada.

The lower regions of states such as Illinois, Indiana, and Ohio were settled largely by southern pioneers. State law forbade those pioneers from holding slaves. Still, many of them were sympathetic to the South. Acting on their old loyalties, they were quick to turn in a runaway. Yet the southern halves of border states also held strongholds of antislavery sentiment. Ripley, Ohio, and Richmond, Indiana, were centers of antislavery activity. Richmond was a major outpost of the Underground

Railroad. A slave on the run in the North lived a life of confusion and fear. Who could a runaway trust? Would a stranger betray him or help him?

Many runaway slaves headed for Canada as their place of final freedom. Canada, a colony of Great Britain, had laws forbidding slavery in any form. It is not known how many African Americans escaped to Canada. Estimates of those who arrived on Canadian soil range between twenty thousand and seventy-five thousand in the years before the Civil War.[16]

Some escapees trekked as far as California, where they worked in the goldfields. Being recaptured in a place as remote as California was almost impossible. Still others found jobs on ships that operated in the open sea. The whaling port of New Bedford, Massachusetts, was an antislavery town where many black sailors lived.

Prime destinations for escapees were to African-American communities in Northern cities. Philadelphia, Boston, and New York all had thriving black neighborhoods. In those cities, a fugitive found protection and friendship. African-American city dwellers formed what they called vigilance committees. These were organizations devoted to helping individuals. The committees organized virtual police forces that kept slave catchers and reward seekers out of their neighborhoods.

New York City's vigilance committee was headed by David Ruggles, an African American who was

$100 REWARD!

RANAWAY

From the undersigned, living on Current River, about twelve miles above Doniphan, in Ripley County, Mo., on 2nd of March, 1860, A NEGRO MAN, about 30 years old, weighs about 160 pounds; high forehead, with a scar on it; had on brown pants and coat very much worn, and an old black wool hat; shoes size No. 11.

The above reward will be given to any person who may apprehend this said negro out of the State; and fifty dollars if apprehended in this State outside of Ripley county, or $25 if taken in Ripley county.

APOS TUCKER.

Wanted posters offering rewards were often posted to entice people to turn in runaway slaves.

born free in 1810. Under Ruggles's leadership, the New York Vigilance Committee protected runaways. The committee found jobs for fugitives, and often paid for lawyers who tried to secure their legal freedom. Ruggles also petitioned New York's political leadership to provide better schools for the city's black children. In Boston, a vigilance committee acted with surprising boldness. On February 15,

1851, a group of twenty or more black men stormed into the Boston courthouse. The men pushed aside the deputies who tried to stop them. Once inside, they took an African-American man, Shadrach Minkins, from a jail cell and hurried him into the streets. Minkins was an escaped slave. He had been arrested that morning by Boston police and was being held for his master. After breaking him out of jail, the committee took Minkins to the house of a white blacksmith in the town of Concord. From there, the fugitive was sent to Vermont and finally to Canada.

To many Americans, the action of the Boston Vigilance Committee was shocking, and it ensured anger in the future. A group of blacks attacking a courthouse and freeing a prisoner was seen as an act of insurrection on a frightening scale. But others thought the Minkins affair was just another step made by the increasingly aggressive antislavery forces in the country. In the 1850s, abolitionist societies increased in numbers and in boldness. The most daring of these abolitionist groups was the Underground Railroad. Its members regularly defied the law and risked their lives to erase the evil of slavery from the land.

CHAPTER Five

The Underground Railroad at Work

"**W**e must trample this law [the Fugitive Slave Law of 1850] underfoot . . . It is not for you to choose whether you will or not obey a law such as this. You are as much under obligation not to obey it, as you are not to lie, steal, or commit murder."[1]

—The Unitarian minister Samuel J. May, addressing his congregation in Syracuse, New York

Stations and Stationmasters

Stations or depots on the Underground Railroad were ordinary households run by antislavery families. They were also called safe houses as a runaway could take temporary shelter in such a house and feel relatively safe. The depots spread northward, ten to twenty miles apart, like links on a chain. Mostly they were farmhouses. Legends say the stations had secret compartments built behind walls where the fugitive could hide from slave catchers. Modern researchers have found few examples of such hidden quarters. Escapees were usually put up in spare bedrooms, in attics, or inside barns.

Often word was sent ahead through messengers that a fugitive or a group of fugitives would soon arrive at a station. Such advanced word was not always possible. In many cases, the escapees hesitantly knocked on a strange door in the middle of the night. Children of the safe houses knew to keep quiet and stay out of the way while their parents tended to the runaways. The children also understood they were not to blab to their neighbors about the comings and goings of the strangers who arrived at night.

In the depots, the escapees—passengers—were allowed to sleep. They were fed and perhaps given a few pennies to buy provisions later on. They were always told how to find the next station, the next link on the chain to freedom. In some cases, passengers were given rides on farm wagons. When riding, they had to hide in the wagons beneath loads of hay.

Jonathan Walker saw himself as a stationmaster, even though he had no permanent house. He was a sailor from New England who owned a small fishing boat. He regularly took escaped slaves northward

The Rokeby Museum in Vermont

The state of Vermont had major Underground Railroad routes that led to Canada. Hundreds of people seeking freedom in Canada stopped at a farmhouse called Rokeby, near the town of Ferrisburgh. The house belonged to the Robinsons, a family of Quaker sheep farmers.

Today the Rokeby farm is open to the public, and visitors see a real station on the Underground Railroad. Robinson family members were energetic letter writers. Hundreds of their letters dating back to slavery days are preserved in the house. Historians study these letters to increase our knowledge of life on the Underground Railroad.

on his vessel. In 1841, Walker agreed to hide seven slaves from Pensacola, Florida, in his boat and transport them to freedom. The boat was caught in a gale and pushed back to shore. Walker was arrested. A Florida judge ordered him to be branded on the hand with the letters "SS" for "slave stealer." Northerners were outraged by the punishment. John Greenleaf Whittier, the abolitionist poet, wrote a poem dedicated to Walker:

> *Then lift that manly right hand,*
> *bold ploughman of the wave!*
> *Its branded palm shall prophecy*
> *"SALVATION TO THE SLAVE."*[2]

Because their work was so dangerous, most stationmasters went about their business in secrecy. Still, a few actually advertised the fact that their house was a station on the Underground Railroad. John Rankin of Ripley, Ohio, left a lantern burning all night outside his house. Rankin wanted escapees to follow the light and find his house easily. An ex-slave named Arnold Gragston said, "Mr. Rankin . . . had a big lighthouse in his yard . . . and he kept it burning all night. It always meant freedom for the slave if he could get to this light."[3] Levi Coffin of Richmond, Indiana, also defied dangers and let it be known that he was a stationmaster. Coffin became

This engraving shows a U.S. marshal branding the hand of Jonathan Walker for helping slaves to escape.

Railroad Stockholders

The Underground Railroad cost very little to operate. All stationmasters were volunteers who collected no pay. Yet some families who ran the safe houses needed money to buy extra food for the fugitives.

Many Americans donated money to the Underground Railroad without working directly for the organization. True to the coded words used by the Railroad, those money donors were called stockholders. The term fit. In the business world, a stockholder finances an operation while not necessarily participating in its work. Stockholders kept their donations a secret because even contributing to what was considered to be a criminal organization was, in itself, a criminal act.

such a famous stationmaster that he is often called the "President of the Underground Railroad."[4]

Coffin was born in the slave state of North Carolina. When he was seven years old, he saw a long line of slaves marching up the road near his house. The slaves were chained together. The man leading them held a whip in his hand. Coffin's father approached one of the slaves and said, "Well, boys, why do they chain you?" The slave answered, "They have taken us away from our wives and children, and they chain us lest we should make our escape and go back to them." Seeing these men treated in such a horrible manner shocked Levi Coffin. He later wrote, "I date my conversion to Abolitionism [to that] incident . . ."[5] In 1826, Coffin moved to Indiana, where he became a prosperous storekeeper. He established safe houses in Newport (present day Fountain City). His wife, Catharine, was as devoted

Levi Coffin

as he was to the Underground Railroad. Over the years, the Coffins helped more than three thousand slaves flee from captivity.[6] Levi and Catharine Coffin are arguably the most successful workers in the history of the Underground Railroad.

The Coffins risked going to jail. They could even be hung for the crime of "theft." Still, they continued to help slaves escape to freedom. Levi Coffin believed his work on the Underground Railroad was protected by God. "As to my safety, my life was in the hands of my Divine Master . . . I had no fear of the danger that seemed to threaten my life and business."[7] Levi Coffin even wrote poetically about being wakened in the middle of the night by bands of ragged, fearful, and starving people. "We knew not what night or what hour of the night we would be roused from slumber by a gentle rap at the door. That was the signal announcing the arrival of a train of the Underground Railroad, for the locomotive did not whistle, not make any unnecessary noise."[8]

The Conductors

Conductors held the most dangerous job of all Underground Railroad workers. They sneaked into plantations, gathered slaves, and took them to the North. Like train conductors, they moved people. Much of their work was done in the Southern states. In the South, patrollers could kill them on the spot. Being arrested by a local sheriff was a frightening experience for a conductor. Southern courts imposed harsh punishments, including death by hanging, upon anyone helping a slave escape.

Many conductors worked for money. They were paid by free family members to escort their people from slave quarters and bring them to freedom. The pay was generally low. The risks a conductor took were extreme.

John Fairfield was a white man, born into a slaveholding family in Virginia. As a child, his best friend was a slave boy named Bill. The two played the usual boyhood games. They also had quiet, secret talks. Though he was just a boy, Fairfield developed a deep hatred of slavery. His friend Bill told him he wished to escape. They made a pact that they would work together and someday Bill would be liberated.

When they were young men, John Fairfield and Bill journeyed to Ohio. Bill acted as if he were Fairfield's slave. An owner and slave traveling together was a common enough practice in the free states. The two played the part perfectly and aroused

The Levi and Catharine Coffin House

A home owned by the Coffins stands today in Fountain City, Indiana. A brick two-story house, it was built in about 1839. The Coffins lived in the house for eight years and in that time helped hundreds of slaves to escape. It is believed that one of the slaves who hid temporarily in the house was the inspiration for Eliza, a runaway slave character in the famous book *Uncle Tom's Cabin*. The Levi Coffin House is now an Indiana State Historic Site and serves as a museum.

no suspicions from the authorities. They journeyed to Canada where Bill could be free. For Bill, the childhood scheme hatched by two boys was now complete. For Fairfield, the work was just beginning. He became one of the boldest conductors on the Underground Railroad.

Fairfield differed from the gentle Quakers who worked for the Railroad. He carried a gun. He sometimes gave rifles to the bands of slaves he took northward. If a fight with patrollers broke out, Fairfield wanted as many gunmen as possible on his side. Being a white Southerner gave him certain advantages. Fairfield knew the ways of the South. He spoke in a genuine Southern accent. Often, he posed as a slave buyer and entered plantations claiming he was looking for prospects to purchase. When leading escapees over Southern roads, he told passersby they were his slaves and he was transporting them to his farm. Sometimes he bought tickets for slaves and rode with them on a train toward the North. A superb actor, Fairfield helped hundreds of slaves to freedom by posing as a slaveholder himself.

The John Fairfield legend grew in the annals of the Underground Railroad. Still, some of his missions in the South went wrong. Several times he was arrested, and he spent many months in jail. A crafty person, he broke out of jail on numerous occasions. Levi Coffin knew Fairfield well and called him a young man "fond of adventure and excitement."[9]

Another famous conductor was Seth Concklin. Like Fairfield, Concklin was a white man. There the similarity between the two ended. Fairfield was refined, elegant, and born into wealth. Concklin was plump, his clothes were always rumpled, and he grew up in poverty in rural New York. Concklin's rough manners and unkempt appearance made him look like a slave catcher or a patroller from the rural South. An excellent actor, he played this role brilliantly.

This oil painting, **Underground Railroad,** *was done by Charles T. Webber in 1893.*

While in Ohio in 1851, Concklin was approached by an escaped slave named Peter Still. The ex-slave wanted Concklin to journey to Alabama and help his wife and three children escape from their plantation. Still gave Concklin about one hundred dollars, his life savings. Concklin got the family out of their slave quarters and to the Tennessee River where he had purchased a small boat. Ahead lay four hundred miles of backbreaking rowing for the party to reach Indiana. Two of the Still boys were strong teenagers who eagerly fell into the task of rowing. When they passed other boats with white crews aboard, Concklin stood and gruffly gave orders to the two teenagers. Giving orders to blacks in rough language was something any Southern patroller would do.

After an exhausting journey, Concklin's party reached Indiana. There, their luck ran out. On a road, they were challenged by a group of white hunters. Concklin claimed he was a slave catcher, leading the blacks back to their owner. This time his act failed. Concklin and the escapees were put in jail. The slave owner was summoned and the entire party was placed on a riverboat to Alabama. The owner threatened Concklin with harsh punishment. Concklin said he was acting as a Christian, and would do the same thing again in a moment. Later Concklin's body was found floating in the river. His hands were tied behind him and his head was crushed. The slave owner told others he probably jumped overboard during the night and was hit by the paddlewheel boat's large paddles. There were no witnesses. The owner was not charged with a crime.

Ironically, Concklin completed his mission even in death. The ex-slave Peter Still traveled to abolitionist meetings telling the tragic story of Seth Concklin. Still must have been an excellent public speaker. He collected five thousand dollars from sympathetic men and women. In 1855, Still used the money to buy freedom for his wife and three children. In 1872 his brother, William Still, published a book, *The Underground Rail Road, A Record* that paid tribute to Seth Concklin.

The Passengers

By the 1840s and 1850s, many slaves knew of the Underground Railroad. Owners did everything possible to keep knowledge of the Railroad from entering slave quarters. But whispered word of the Railroad seeped into even the most well-guarded plantations. The Underground Railroad offered the hope of freedom. Still, the act of escape required great courage.

Most escapees operated entirely on their own during the initial stage of their flight. They had to outrun dogs. They were forced to sleep in mosquito-infested swamps or forests. If the night skies were cloudy and they could not see the North

Star, they risked getting lost. Becoming lost often led to being recaptured. When returned to their owners, runaways faced terrible punishments. They were flogged. They were branded with red-hot irons. Some were forced to wear iron collars and bells around their necks to alert owners if they tried to run away again.

The road to freedom held overwhelming dangers. One Underground Railroad worker who helped rescue fugitives coming up through Kentucky wrote:

> Every night of the year saw runaways making their way slyly to the country north. Traps and snares were set for them, into which they fell by the hundreds and were returned to their homes. But once they were infected with the spirit of freedom, they would try again and again . . .[10]

Though many runaways were caught and punished, they fled again and again. Faith in God and a hunger for freedom drove them to escape. They looked upon the Northern states or Canada as the Promised Land of the Bible. To the north lay Canaan, where Moses of old led the Hebrew children. A favorite slave song said:

O Canaan, sweet Canaan
I am bound for the land of Canaan[11]

CHAPTER Six

Black Workers on the Underground Railroad

"Slaveholders pride themselves upon being honorable men; but if you were to hear the enormous lies they tell their slaves, you would have small respect for their veracity [truthfulness] . . . When they visit the North and return home, they tell their slaves of the runaways they have seen, and describe them to be in the most deplorable condition."[1]

> —*Harriet Ann Jacobs, from her 1861 book*
> Incidents in the Life of a Slave Girl

Special Dangers, Special Rewards

Most slaves made their break for freedom without the help of the Underground Railroad.[2] They were too fearful to accept help from anyone—black or white. Turning in a runaway earned a reward of fifty dollars or more. Rarely did a farm family see that much money in one lump sum. The slave on the run knew of the rewards, and shunned strangers as much as possible.

Still, at some point, even the most resourceful escapee needed to seek help. Assistance often came from fellow slaves. A starving and exhausted fugitive felt safer approaching a slave cabin than a house owned by a white or even by a free black. The runaway reasoned a slave would take pity on him and aid his attempt to escape. Slaves, too, collected rewards for turning in a fugitive, yet a hungry person on the run felt safer approaching a slave cabin. Fellow slaves often shared food with runaways. They told him or her of a good spot in the woods to use as a hiding spot while moving northward.

On large plantations, slaves developed secret communications with runaways. One lamp burning in front of a cabin at night might have meant it was safe for the fugitive to enter. Two lamps meant a slave catcher lurked nearby. Certain gospel songs sung on Sunday also spelled the message of safety or danger for a slave hiding in the swamps. Few details of these codes are known today.

Most instances of slaves helping fugitives went unrecorded. Any slave household that sheltered a runaway risked terrible punishment. Because their

Free blacks who were sailors sometimes helped slaves escape to the North by ship.

activity was secret, slaves did not consider their cabins to be stations on the Underground Railroad. A white Ohio abolitionist named James Birney often received slaves who had escaped from the South with the help of other slaves. Birney wrote, "Such matters are almost uniformly managed by the colored people. I know nothing of them till they are passed."[3]

Many blacks, both slaves and free, worked as sailors. In their capacity as seamen, they were able to hide slaves on board their ships. Taking flight on ships appealed to slaves from the Deep South. In states such as Mississippi and Louisiana, a walk to the free states of the North required many months of travel through dangerous countryside. One escapee spent a full year walking from Alabama to Ohio. Ships offered a safer method of escape. Frederick Douglass made his flight partway by ship. Douglass called ships "freedom's swift-winged angels, that fly round the world."[4]

Here, Ellen Kraft is depicted in the clothes she wore for her escape disguised as a man in 1854.

Acting entirely on their own, slaves devised ingenious methods of taking flight. William and Ellen Craft were a married couple who lived as slaves in Georgia. In 1848, they planned an escape using the railroad—not the underground one. Ellen was light skinned enough to pass for white. As part of their escape scheme, she dressed as a young, white gentleman. Because Ellen's facial features were womanly she wrapped a white cloth around her cheeks. She claimed she suffered from a terrible toothache, and the cloth was a bandage. William Craft served as his "master's" trusted servant. William was especially diligent in seeing to his "master's" every need because "he" was in such pain due to the "toothache." The trick worked. Riding the regular train, the Crafts reached Philadelphia and liberty.

Slaves and Ex-Slaves as Agents and Workers

In 1858, a free black man named Daniel Mackey of Maryland helped a slave called Tom to escape. The slave's owner posted a two-hundred-dollar reward for Tom's capture. The fugitive was found, and the owner paid the reward. Daniel Mackey was arrested for the crime of helping a slave "to escape and runaway."[5] Mackey, though he was legally a free man, was sentenced to slavery. He was sold by the sheriff of Talbot County to a slave dealer for the sum of nine hundred fifty dollars. The sheriff then gave two hundred dollars of Mackey's sale price to the owner of the slave Mackey helped to free. The two hundred dollars was compensation for the reward money the owner had to pay to retrieve his escapee.[6]

Black workers on the Underground Railroad faced far graver dangers than whites. They could be imprisoned, enslaved, or executed. In court, a black person's testimony meant little when balanced against that of a white slave catcher. Yet African Americans served as stationmasters, conductors, and in all sorts of other positions on the Underground Railroad. Thousands more who were not members of the Underground Railroad still did their part to help slaves escape captivity.

Henry Bibb was born in Kentucky in 1815. His father was a state senator and prosperous white farmer. His mother was a black slave. State laws determining freeborn and slave babies followed the mother. Because Bibb's mother was a slave, he, too, was a slave. However, nothing could keep him bound in a life of slavery. "Among other good trades I learned the art of running away to perfection."[7]

With the help of the Underground Railroad, Bibb fled. He returned to Kentucky as a conductor with hopes to free his wife and child. Bibb was captured and recaptured, often being brutally whipped; each time, he escaped. Once, a fellow slave betrayed him for a five-dollar reward. Worst of all, his wife lost all hope of gaining freedom and became the mistress

The Peter Mott House, a Monument to Freedom

In Lawnside, New Jersey, stands the historic Peter Mott House. Built in the 1840s, the house belonged to a free African-American businessman and farmer named Peter Mott. It once served as a station on the Underground Railroad. Mott was an ordained minister. He and his wife risked their freedom by allowing fleeing slaves to stay at the farmhouse. In modern times, the two-story house was abandoned, and authorities considered demolishing the old structure. The house was saved by history lovers and students of the Underground Railroad. It was officially opened as a museum of the Underground Railroad on October 13, 2001. At the dedication, a local historian named Linda Waller Shockley said, "The Underground Railroad was a system committed to the human desire for freedom."[8]

of her owner. Bibb never saw his wife and daughter again. He finally successfully escaped to Detroit, where he married again and had another child.

After the Fugitive Slave Act was passed in 1850, Bibb fled northward to Canada to avoid capture and settled in Toronto. There, he was an enthusiastic supporter of the Underground Railroad. He received fugitives the Railroad brought to Toronto. Bibb helped the escapees find jobs and gave them emergency money. He also established a newspaper called *Voice of the Fugitive.* The paper served as an official voice of the Underground Railroad. Though he had no formal education, Bibb became a powerful writer and antislavery spokesman. When it came to condemning slavery, he said, "If I had a thousand tongues, I could find useful employment for them all."[9]

William Still led no daring escapes and faced no unusual dangers. Yet his name is honored in the Underground Railroad. Still was born a free person in New Jersey. Because his family was poor, he had to learn reading and writing on his own. In 1847, he was given a job as a clerk and janitor at the Pennsylvania Society for the Abolition of Slavery in Philadelphia. He rose rapidly to become the society's leading counselor and helper of fugitives. Escaped slaves appealing for assistance usually saw

William Still was an African-American reformer who was secretary of the Philadelphia Anti-Slavery Society and author of *The Underground Rail Road.*

Still first. Still came from a family of eighteen children, some of whom were born into slavery. While interviewing one escapee, he discovered the man was his brother, whom he had never met before.

Still became the unofficial historian of the Underground Railroad. In 1872, he published a book called *The Underground Rail Road*. The book was a history of the organization that he served. In the book, Still says little about himself. He tells the stories of railroad people as if those men and women were simply going about their everyday jobs. Today, historians value Still's book as a prime source of information about the Underground Railroad.

Jermain Loguen was born a slave in Tennessee. At a young age, he and two friends escaped and headed north toward Canada. Along the way, they met a white man named Ross who forged papers that said they were free blacks. The white man also told them of houses on the road whose owners were friendly to runaways. Loguen never forgot this act of kindness extended by a stranger. He determined that he, too, would assist slaves trying to reach freedom.

Loguen later settled in Syracuse, New York. He went to school, learned to read, and became a minister at the African Methodist Episcopal Zion Church. He also let it be known that his house was a depot on the Underground Railroad. Loguen even had a business card printed up that identified him as an "Underground Railroad Agent."[10] During the 1850s, he and his wife received some fifteen hundred fugitives, and they aided them on their march toward Canada.[11] The couple took in runaways even while their thirteen-year-old daughter lay in their home dying of tuberculosis.

A daring Underground Railroad conductor was John P. Parker. He wrote about his work in the book *His Promised Land.* Parker lived in Ohio and regularly escorted slaves out of Kentucky. One night he was told of a group of fugitive slaves hiding in the Kentucky woods about twenty miles to the south. Parker wrote:

> I volunteered to go to the rescue. As my mission was a dangerous one, I put a pair of pistols in my pockets and a knife in my belt . . . That night we found the party in the midst of the deep woods, scared and perfectly helpless. There were ten in all, which included two women and their husbands . . . They were so badly demoralized some of them wanted to give themselves up . . . One of the men set up a wail when I had them ready to start. Drawing a pistol I sternly gave him the choice of picking up his things and coming along, or being shot down in cold blood.[12]

The party made their way northward trying to maintain silence. Parker complained that they "were hopeless woodsmen" because they made too much noise as they walked. While resting, one man sneaked off to get a drink at a brook. Parker heard a shout. Soon the man "came racing through the brush pursued by two white men." Parker made the rest of his party lie still. A shot rang out. "Shortly there was a cracking of the brush. Peering cautiously through the bushes, I saw our man being led by a rope. He had his arms tied behind his back." Parker prayed silently that the captured fugitive would not give up the group's hiding place. The man did not reveal where the fugitives hid, and Parker continued leading the trek.[13]

At the banks of the Ohio River, Parker found a boat. He could see the lights of Ripley, Ohio, on the far side. ". . . but they [the lights] might as well have been [on] the moon so far as being a relief to me."[14] Suddenly Parker heard dogs barking. He knew the patrollers were not far behind. The boat he found was too small to carry the whole party. Two of the men had to stay behind. As the boat started off, a woman screamed that one of the men left on the riverbank was her husband. Her screams became hysterical and pierced the night. Because of the noise, the rescue mission seemed doomed. Parker wrote in his memoir:

> Then I witnessed an example of heroism and self-sacrifice that made me proud of my race. For one of the single men safely in the boat, hearing the cry of the woman for her husband, arose without a word [and] walked quietly to the bank. The husband sprang into the boat as I pushed off.[15]

Parker's book, *His Promised Land*, contains many stories of bravery and rescue. Although the book was written more than one hundred years ago, it is exciting reading to this day.

Frederick Douglass

At twelve years old, the slave boy Frederick Douglass met an Irish sailor on the Baltimore docks. "Are ye a slave for life?" the sailor asked. Douglass told him that, indeed, he was a slave for life. Later Douglass wrote, "The good Irishman seemed to be deeply affected by [my] statement . . . He said it was a shame to hold me. [He] advised me to run away to the north; that I should find friends there, and that I should be free." Douglass did not, immediately, take the man's advice. At age twelve, he was not ready to begin life as a fugitive. Besides, he was wary of all whites. "White men have been known to encourage slaves to escape, and then, to get the reward, catch them and return them to their masters," Douglass wrote.[16] Still, the idea that he could escape and then find friends in the North intrigued him. With the help of friends, he could build a new life.

Frederick Douglass was the leading black abolitionist in the country. He was a former slave who had run away to the North.

When he was sixteen, Douglass was sold to a plantation owner in Maryland. He was already known as a defiant slave, one not afraid to talk back to his owner. The plantation owner sent Douglass to a farmer who was also a "slave breaker." In Douglass's words, the foreman was a "nigger-breaker."[17] This meant he was hired by slave owners to tie up and whip slaves who exhibited any sort of an independent spirit. The whippings were designed to be so savage they beat the spirit out of even the most rebellious slave.

Douglass endured the whippings, and he fought back. Once, he had an actual fistfight with the overseer and left the man's face bloodied. Perhaps out of fear, the foreman quit punishing the young slave. Douglass later wrote, "The battle with Mr. Covey [the foreman] was the turning-point in my career as a slave . . . My long-crushed spirit rose . . . I now resolved that, however long I might remain a slave in form, the day had passed forever when I could be a slave in fact."[18]

At age twenty-one, Douglass escaped. He journeyed to New Bedford, Massachusetts, where he worked on ships.

In 1841, he delivered a stirring speech to the Massachusetts Anti-Slavery Society. From that point on, he was in demand as a speaker. He traveled to abolitionist meetings throughout the North, exciting the men and women with his inspirational talks. He also fought for equal rights for free African-American workers and students.

Douglass settled in Rochester, New York, where his house was a depot on the Underground Railroad. He helped many fugitives escape to Canada.

Douglass never made his Underground Railroad activities public. In fact, he deplored such attention:

> I have never approved of the very public manner in which some of our western friends have conducted what they call the underground railroad, but which, I think, by their open declarations, has been made most emphatically the upperground railroad.[19]

Douglass applauded the bravery of those agents who openly boasted of their activity, but he was afraid such boasts would tip off the slave catcher on the hunt. "I would [rather] keep the merciless slave-holder profoundly ignorant of the means of flight adopted by the slave . . . Let him [the slaveholder] be left to feel his way in the dark . . ."[20]

As a writer, a speaker, and an Underground Railroad agent, Douglass emerged as one of the nation's most powerful abolitionists. He fulfilled the vision he had as a boy when he dreamed he could build a new life in the North with the help of friends. His closest friends were fellow abolitionists Levi Coffin, William Still, Wendell Phillips, William Lloyd Garrison, and John Brown. During the Civil War, Douglass discussed the issue of slavery with President Abraham Lincoln. Douglass helped persuade Northern leaders to use black troops in battle. By the end of the war, more than 186,000 blacks served in the Union Army.[21] Many historians have concluded that the addition of

African-American soldiers tipped the balance of forces to the Northern side.

Throughout his life, Douglass exhibited the spirit of a man yearning for freedom. As a slave boy, he once stood gazing at the ships tied up to a Baltimore dock. Like a preacher in a pulpit, he cried out to the ships:

> O God, save me! God deliver me! Let me be free! Is there any God? Why am I a slave? I will run away. I will not stand it. Get caught or get clear . . . I have only one life to lose. . . . I will take to the water. This very bay shall bear me into freedom . . . There is a better day coming.[22]

CHAPTER *Seven*

Harriet Tubman: The Moses of Her People

Go down, Moses,
Way down in Egypt land.
Tell ole Pharaoh
Let my people go.[1]

—A spiritual often sung
by Harriet Tubman

A Slave Childhood

Harriet Tubman never knew the exact date or even the year of her birth. Rarely was the birth of a slave child written down, neither in family nor in church record books. She was born and grew up in Dorchester County, Maryland. Her name at birth was Araminta Ross. She later changed her name to

Along with helping runaway slaves, Harriet Tubman was also a spy for the Union Army during the Civil War.

Harriet, after her mother. In 1844, she married John Tubman, a free black man. She took the name Harriet Tubman to greatness as a conductor on the Underground Railroad.

Tubman once said, "I grew up like a neglected weed—ignorant of liberty, having no experience of it."[2] She was the fifth of at least nine children in her family.[3] A neighboring white woman employed her at age five as a baby-sitter. Gently she rocked the baby's cradle, but the baby still cried. When the baby cried, the white woman beat Harriet. Often she suffered several beatings in the course of a day. Night after night, Harriet cried herself to sleep.

Still, Harriet Tubman considered herself to be fortunate. She was never sold to some distant farm. So she was able to visit her family at least on Sundays. Being sold remained the greatest agony a slave could endure. As Harriet grew up, the cotton industry expanded in the Deep South. Many slaves in the eastern part of the country were sold to the feared "Georgia Traders."[4] Harriet saw two of her sisters sold to slave traders and driven in chains to the Deep South. The girls and their parents broke into tears at the sight. Harriet developed a terror that someday she too would be sold to some slave trader. "Every time I saw a white man I was afraid of being carried away."[5]

Young Harriet was often "hired out" by her owner. That meant she was sent to neighboring households to wash and iron clothes, scrub floors, and cook. Her owner was paid for her services. She, as a slave, never received a penny. Later, her owner sent her to the woods to chop trees and haul lumber. She was one of the few slaves who preferred such fieldwork to household duties. She enjoyed the outdoors, smelling the grasses and feeling the dew. Through working in the woods, she developed extraordinary muscles. Her strength surprised her overseers as well as her fellow slaves. Though barely five feet tall, she was able to move lumber as well as any man.

When not working, Harriet Tubman prayed and lost herself in religious thought. She never learned how to read and write. Therefore, she could not read the stories in the Bible herself. Instead, she committed Biblical verses to memory—word for word. In future years, Tubman became the boldest of all conductors on the Underground Railroad. She faced grave dangers as she led people out of captivity. Always she relied on her faith in God to give her courage.

When Tubman was about twelve years old, an ugly incident changed her life. She was in a general store near her home when an angry white overseer burst through the door. The overseer was looking for a slave who had walked off the job without permission. He spotted the man. The slave tried to run. The overseer picked up a lead weight and threw it at the slave. Acting as a shield, Harriet stepped between the slave and the overseer. The weight hit her in the head full force. "[It] broke my skull and cut a piece [of my hat] clean off and drove it into my head."[6]

For weeks Tubman lay in her bed, hovering between life and death. She recovered, but the thrown lead weight left her with a lifelong sleeping sickness. Modern historians speculate the blow induced the disease epilepsy within her. She would fall asleep suddenly, without being able to stop herself. The sleeping spells came without warning in the middle of the day, during work, or during a conversation. Miraculously, the spells did not hamper her work as a conductor on the Underground Railroad.

Escape!

In 1849, Harriet's owner died. She became convinced she would soon be sold by the owner's wife who inherited all the slaves on the farm. Harriet and two of her brothers ran away. Their escape attempt failed miserably. The fugitives vaguely knew that Pennsylvania was a free state and they could walk there by following the North Star. But the night was cloudy, obscuring all the stars in the heavens. The three argued about directions. Finally, the small band gave up and headed home.

Tubman remained determined that she must break free. She later said she was inspired by glorious dreams. In dreams she was ". . . flying over fields and towns, and rivers and mountains, looking down upon them 'like a bird' and reaching at last a great fence."[7] In the fall of 1849, she tried to escape again, this time on her own. Moving mostly at night, she began a perilous one hundred-mile journey toward Pennsylvania.[8] When she could not see the North Star, she imagined she was being led by a pillar of fire. She believed the fire was the same mysterious light that once guided Moses out of Egypt.

From the beginning of her flight, she had decided to accept help if help was offered. She knew from secret conversations with other slaves there were farmhouses on the road northward whose owners helped runaways. Her first stop was at the home of a white Quaker woman. The woman gave her a piece of paper to introduce her to the next house farther north. In this manner she made her way, house by house, to the Pennsylvania border. Emerging into the free state was, to her, a miracle delivered by a loving God. "When I found I had crossed that line I looked at my hands to see if I were the same person. There was such a glory over everything; the sun came like gold through the trees and over the fields, and I felt like I was in Heaven."[9]

Tubman settled in Philadelphia, which at the time supported one of the largest communities of

This painting by Paul Collins shows Harriet Tubman leading the way for a number of escaped slaves.

free African Americans in the country. This was her first experience with freedom and she marveled at the sensation. She could actually walk city streets and go where she wished without a slave boss supervising her every move. Philadelphia, like every American city at the time, was segregated. Blacks maintained their own neighborhoods and institutions separate from whites. Schools and churches, founded by blacks, served their community.

A Slave's Greatest Fear

Harriet Tubman made her escape largely because she was afraid of being sold to strangers. Slaves relied on their families to provide comfort and security in their cruel world. Being sold tore a person away from his or her family.

The strong family ties developed by slaves can be seen in this grim story that was told in an antislavery pamphlet that circulated during Tubman's time:

> One woman was told by a slave dealer who lived near her, that he had bought her; she said, "Have you bought my husband?" "No." "Have you bought my children?" "No." She said no more, but went into the court-yard, took an axe, and with her right hand chopped off her left. She then returned to the house as if nothing had happened, and told her purchaser she was ready to go; but a one-handed slave being of little value, she was left with her children.[10]

By no means was Philadelphia a paradise for the blacks. Racial strife often rocked the city. Gangs of whites fought gangs of blacks on the streets. A year after Tubman's escape, Congress passed the Fugitive Slave Law. The law allowed slave catchers to roam about Philadelphia rounding up any black they suspected was a fugitive.

Harriet found work in her new city. Most often she toiled in kitchens. She was free, although she had to keep a watchful eye out for slave catchers and police in general. Naturally, she felt lonely in her new life. "I was free, but there was no one to welcome me to the land of freedom. I was a stranger in a strange land."[11] Often she thought of her parents, brothers, and sisters still held in slavery. "I was free, and they should be free."[12]

In 1850, Harriet Tubman made her way back to Maryland. Once in her home state, she liberated her niece who was about to be sold to the Deep South. Several months later, she returned and smuggled out her brother and two other men. Few details are known about these early missions. Probably she enlisted the help of safe houses on the Underground Railroad. She had attended abolitionist meetings in Philadelphia and knew more about the Railroad's activities. Those early journeys into the land of slavery demonstrated her courage and her determination. She had lived as a free person for less than two years. She treasured her freedom as if it were a gift granted by heaven. Yet she risked everything by returning to a slave state in order to bestow the gift of freedom to others. In so doing, she believed she was heeding a powerful voice from above—"The Lord who told me to do this."[13]

The Queen of the Underground Railroad

Harriet Tubman made at least nineteen trips to the South and liberated more than three hundred slaves.[14] Often she led the slaves directly to Canada because she could no longer trust that they would be safe in the United States after the Fugitive Slave Law of 1850. In her rescue missions, she stopped at established stations on the Underground Railroad. She also developed a network of safe houses owned by blacks. The names of the black households who harbored Tubman and her fugitives have long been forgotten by history.

Her exploits into slave states became the stuff of legends. Showing both courage and intelligence, she rose as the Underground Railroad's most famous conductor. Tubman tolerated no whimpering or cowardice from her passengers. She brought a gun with her on many missions. When one man lost heart and said he wanted to return to his owner, Tubman pointed the gun at his head and said simply, "Move or die."[15] Often she led fugitives in broad daylight down public streets. It was common enough

Harriet Tubman (far left) poses in 1900 with some of the former slaves that she helped escape.

for an owner to let a trusted slave lead a group to a particular destination. Once, at a train station where she suspected slave catchers were watching her, she put her party on a southward-bound train. This act fooled the slave catchers because they could not believe that anyone escaping from Maryland would head south.

She became a hated figure among Maryland slave owners. A forty thousand-dollar reward was put on her head.[16] Because of this gigantic reward, slave catchers and patrollers everywhere hunted for her. The slave catchers knew her habits. For example, it was well known she could not read and write. At one point, when she feared slave catchers were nearby, she sat in a public place reading a book. Seeing a free black lady who could read was not terribly unusual. However, everyone knew that Harriet Tubman was illiterate. So, to cast suspicions away from her, she gazed at the book intensely as if absorbed by the story. All the time she prayed she was not holding the book upside down.

Slave catchers studied her picture on "Wanted" posters. The picture was sketched by an artist and based on descriptions of her features. Therefore, one would think she would be easily recognized in Maryland. But some reports say Harriet Tubman was able to use her facial muscles to alter her features. She could make herself look years older. She could also feign the faraway look of an empty-headed or an insane person. One characteristic she could not disguise was her sleeping sickness. Without warning, even while leading a party to freedom, she was likely to fall into a deep sleep. The fugitives in her care had no choice but to wait until she woke up. Amazingly, the trance-like bouts of sleeping sickness never betrayed her. In the course of her work, she never lost a passenger to capture. The famous Quaker abolitionist Thomas Garrett once said of her, "Harriet seems to have a special angel to guide her on her journey of mercy."[17]

When not rescuing slaves, Tubman lived in Philadelphia and in Canada. She worked at low-paid jobs and rarely spent the few pennies she earned. She used her savings to finance her missions as a conductor. During the course of her missions, she met famous Underground Railroad figures such as Frederick Douglass, William Still, and John Brown. She was a valued speaker at abolitionist meetings. When giving lectures, she told of her rescues in exciting detail. Audiences sat, spellbound, listening to every word. Said one listener, "The most refined person would listen for hours while she related intensely interesting incidents in her life, told in the simplest manner, but always seasoned with good taste."[18] Stories about Harriet Tubman's work in rescuing slaves were told everywhere—in the North as well as in the South. Americans grew to admire her as a fearless, smart, and strong woman. Everywhere, she was called Moses because she led her people out of bondage. In 1913, an African-American newspaper dubbed Tubman the "Queen of the Underground."[19]

War and Beyond

Early in the Civil War years, Harriet Tubman sailed with Northern troops to the Sea Islands off the shore of South Carolina. These islands were occupied by the North starting in 1862. By this time, she was a celebrated figure. One observer noted that Northern officers "never failed to tip their caps when meeting her."[20] The Sea Islands region was hot, swampy, and infested with mosquitoes. Many soldiers stationed there came down with the dreaded disease malaria. Tubman treated those soldiers with her own medicines composed of herbs and roots. Treating people with special plant products was another skill she had acquired over the years.

Acting under orders from Union officers, Tubman repeatedly sneaked behind Confederate lines. She used the tricks she learned as a conductor on the Underground Railroad to scout deep into enemy territory. She was not so well known by Southerners in the Deep South. Therefore, she was able to travel in the guise of an ordinary slave woman. Behind the lines, she served as a spy and reported on Confederate military movements. She made contact with many South Carolina slaves. In June 1863, she helped execute a daring raid. The raid allowed Union boats to spirit away more than seven hundred slaves from two wealthy South Carolina plantations.[21] This mass liberation of slaves robbed the South of the plantations' valuable crops. News of the incredible raid was passed on to the Northern states and the esteem of "Moses" Tubman soared to even greater heights.

Harriet Tubman sits in a chair at her home in Auburn, New York, in 1911.

After the Civil War, Tubman established schools in North Carolina. Her inability to read and write had hampered her all her life. She hoped to bring the gift of literacy to all children. Tubman continued her work as a public speaker. Often she spoke before women's rights groups. Tubman settled in Auburn, New York where she founded a home for elderly African Americans. Harriet Tubman died in Auburn on March 10, 1913. She was probably ninety-three years old. No one knew her precise age because her birth, as a slave, was not recorded in any books.

Harriet Tubman, the Queen of the Underground Railroad and the Moses of her People, was born a slave. She lived to see slavery ended in the United States. Her courage and her determination helped to rid the country of slavery, its greatest evil. Freedom, she believed, was her God-given destiny even though she was a slave at birth. Harriet Tubman once said, "I had reasoned this out in my mind; there was one of two things I had a right to, liberty or death; if I could not have one, I would have the other."[22]

CHAPTER Eight

Free at Last!

"**A** house divided against itself cannot stand. I believe this government cannot endure, permanently half slave and half free."[1]

—Abraham Lincoln, speaking in 1858

War and Emancipation

By the late 1850s, clashes between proslavery and antislavery Americans began to tear the country apart. Arguments for and against slavery often took a religious tone. One side pointed to the Bible and said God condoned and even blessed the practice of slavery. The other side pointed to scriptures and insisted God condemned slavery as a sin. At times, the two sides cited the same Biblical chapter and verse *and even the same sentence* to prove their points.

As the arguments over slavery heated up, violent confrontations raged at every level of American society. Fistfights and worse broke out, even in the United States Congress. Because they feared attack, congressmen began carrying guns to their offices. Said one senator, "The only persons who do not have a revolver . . . are those who have two revolvers."[2]

Senator Preston Brooks of South Carolina uses a cane to beat Senator Charles Sumner of Maryland during an antislavery debate in 1856.

Remembering the Underground Railroad

The heroic work of the Underground Railroad is recalled today in museums and historic sites. The National Underground Railroad Freedom Center opened in 2004 is in Cincinnati, Ohio. Exhibits and events at the Freedom Center show how escapees and railroad agents worked at their often dangerous tasks. Scattered throughout the country are houses and churches that were once used as stations on the Underground Railroad and now stand as museums. Ohio leads all other states with thirteen recognized historic sites associated with the Underground Railroad.[3]

Visitors listen to a story about the "Slave Pen" (in background) at the National Underground Railroad Freedom Center.

At the top, slaves flee a southern plantation at night to reach Union lines in this engraving. A Union gun-boat, far out at sea, will offer some protection. At the bottom, fugitive slaves ford the Rappahannock River in Virginia in August 1862 in this colorized photo.

Free at Last!

In the fall of 1860, Abraham Lincoln of Illinois was elected president of the United States. Lincoln was not an abolitionist. He had no plans to immediately free all the slaves in the country. He hoped that slavery would simply fade away and die a natural death. He was, however, adamantly opposed to allowing slavery in the new states opening to the west. Despite his rather mild views on slavery, the people in the South hated Lincoln. They believed he was an abolitionist or even worse. Some speculated that Lincoln would encourage the slaves to rise up, and rampage and riot in the South.

The results of the presidential election of 1860 was the final step on the path toward civil war. In December 1860, the state of South Carolina voted to secede (separate itself) from the rest of the United States. By the time Lincoln was sworn in as president, six other Southern states had also seceded from the American Union. Before the end of 1861, four other states seceded—Virginia, North Carolina, Texas, and Arkansas. The separated Southern states formed the Confederacy, which stood against the Union (the Northern states). Thus, the country split into two opposite and belligerent forces.

On April 12, 1861, Confederate guns from the shore fired on Fort Sumter in the harbor of Charleston, South Carolina. Fort Sumter was a federal facility. The attack plunged the nation into the great Civil War, which raged from April 1861 to May 1865.

The Civil War was one of the bloodiest conflicts fought in American history. But the war accomplished two goals: It reunited the American Union and it freed the slaves. On January 1, 1863, while the war was still being fought, President Lincoln issued the Emancipation Proclamation. The document declared freedom for all slaves in Confederate states that still waged war against the Union. The Emancipation Proclamation was an important first step in ending slavery. In 1865, immediately after the war, Congress approved the Thirteenth Amendment to the Constitution. This amendment finally abolished the practice of slavery in the United States.

The end of slavery marked the final chapter of the Underground Railroad. For decades, Railroad members risked their lives and their freedom to grant freedom to others. The cold words of slavery laws condemned Railroad workers as criminals. Yet the men and women of the Underground Railroad maintained they obeyed a higher law—God's law— which said all people deserve to be free. History has sided with the Underground Railroad. We now celebrate the Railroad workers as grand crusaders of American freedom.

Timeline

1619	The first Africans arrive at the English colony of Jamestown in present-day Virginia; initially the black servants are not classified as slaves.
1741	A slave revolt is brutally suppressed in the New York colony.
1775	The first abolitionist society is established in Philadelphia.
1775–1791	The American Revolutionary War is fought, which results in a separation from England and the establishment of the United States; slavery continues in the country, although the practice begins to fade in the North.
1791	Slaves revolt on the island of Haiti and establish an independent nation under their leader Toussaint L'Ouverture.
1793	Eli Whitney invents the cotton gin, which makes the cotton industry highly profitable, but the new machine prolongs slavery as a consequence.
1808	The United States abolishes the importation of slaves from other countries.

1820	Ex-president Thomas Jefferson writes a famous letter saying slavery is upsetting and alarming the American people like "a firebell in the night."
1822	A potential slave revolt led by Denmark Vesey is put down in South Carolina.
1830– 1840	A network of Underground Railroad stations has been established in the border states and in New England.
1831	A revolution led by the slave Nat Turner is defeated in Virginia; many whites were killed in the uprising, and it resulted in stricter laws governing the lives of slaves and free blacks.
1839	Slaves mutiny and take over the ship *La Amistad*; the rebellious slaves are later freed by a Massachusetts court.
1849	Harriet Tubman escapes from slavery and begins a life as a conductor on the Underground Railroad.
1850	The Compromise of 1850 allows slavery to extend into some western states; the Fugitive Slave Law calls for criminal punishment for anyone helping a slave to escape.
1852	Harriet Beecher Stowe publishes her antislavery classic *Uncle Tom's Cabin*.

1857	In the *Dred Scott* v. *Sandford* decision, the Supreme Court claims that blacks are not citizens of the United States and have no rights in court.
1859	The abolitionist John Brown raids the arsenal at Harpers Ferry, Virginia (today in West Virginia) and tries to start a nationwide slave revolt.
1860	Abraham Lincoln is elected president after a bitter campaign; South Carolina secedes from the Union.
1861	Southern forces fire on Fort Sumter starting the Civil War.
1863	President Lincoln issues the Emancipation Proclamation, an important first step to ending slavery.
1865	The Civil War ends; the Thirteenth Amendment to the U.S. Constitution officially abolishes slavery in the United States.

CHAPTER *Notes*

CHAPTER 1. **Escape of Tice Davids**

1 | George Hendrick and Willene Hendrick eds., *Fleeing for Freedom: Stories of the Underground Railroad As Told by Levi Coffin and William Still* (Chicago: Ivan R. Dee Publishers, 2004), p. 3.

CHAPTER 2. **A Firebell in the Night**

1 | Bruno Leone ed., *Slavery: Opposing Viewpoints* (San Diego, Calif.: Greenhaven Press, 1992), p. 93.

2 | John Hope Franklin and Afred A. Moss, Jr., *From Slavery to Freedom: A History of African Americans* (New York: McGraw Hill, 1994), p. 56.

3 | Ibid., p. 61.

4 | Samuel Eliot Morison, *The Oxford History of the American People* (New York: Oxford University Press, 1965), p. 149

5 | Ibid., p. 149.

6 | Franklin and Moss, p. 76.

7 | Ibid., p. 77.

8 | Peter Kolchin, *American Slavery: 1619–1877* (New York: Hill and Wang Publishers, 2003), p. 3.

9 | Franklin and Moss, p. 76.

10 | Kolchin, p. 95.

11 | Herb Boyd ed., *Autobiography of a People: Three Centuries of African American History Told by*

Those Who Lived It (New York: Doubleday, 2000), p. 71.

12 | Ibid., p. 72.

13 | John P. Parker, *His Promised Land* (New York: W.W. Norton & Company, 1996), p. 26.

14 | Franklin and Moss, p. 118.

15 | Harriet Beecher Stowe, *The Key to Uncle Tom's Cabin, 1854* <http://www.iath.virginia.edu/utc/uncletom/key/keyt.html> (May 29, 2007).

16 | The Annals of America, vol. 4 (Chicago and London: Encyclopedia Brittanica, Inc., 1976), p. 603.

CHAPTER 3. Striking Back at Slavery

1 | John Bassingame ed., *Slave Testimony: Two centuries of Letters, Speeches, Interviews, and Autobiographies* (Baton Rouge: Louisiana State University Press, 1977), p. 50.

2 | David W. Blight ed., *Passages to Freedom: The Underground Railroad in History and Memory* (Washington: Smithsonian Books, 2004), p. 100.

3 | The Annals of America, vol. 8, (Chicago and London: Encyclopedia Brittanica, Inc., 1976), p. 203.

4 | Ibid., p. 203.

5 | Ira Berlin, *Generations of Captivity: A History of African American Slaves* (Cambridge, Mass.: Harvard University Press, 2003), p. 204.

6 | Ira Berlin, Marc Favreau, and Steven F. Mill, eds., *Remembering Slavery: African Americans Talk About Their Personal Experiences of Slavery and Freedom* (New York: The New Press, 1998), p. 145.

7 | Peter Kolchin, *American Slavery: 1619–1877* (New York: Hill and Wang Publishers, 2003), p. 156.

8 | Bruno Leone ed., *Slavery: Opposing Viewpoints* (San Diego, Calif.: Greenhaven Press, 1992), p. 146–147.

9 | Jules Abels, *Man on Fire* (New York: Macmillan, 1971), pp. 390–391.

10 | John Hope Franklin and Afred A. Moss, Jr., *From Slavery to Freedom: A History of African Americans* (New York: McGraw Hill, 1994), p. 173.

11 | Frederick Douglass, *Narrative of the Life of Frederick Douglass, an American Slave* (New York: The Modern Library, 2000), p. 50.

CHAPTER 4. The Hunted and the Hunters: Early Escapees

1 | Frederick Douglass, *Narrative of the Life of Frederick Douglass, an American Slave* (New York: The Modern Library, 2000), p. 49.

2 | Fergus M. Bordewich, *Bound for Canaan: The Underground Railroad and the War for the Soul of America* (New York: Harper Collins, 2005), p. 121.

3 | Ibid., p. 121.

4 | James W. C. Pennington, *The Fugitive Blacksmith, 1849* <http://docsouth.unc.edu/neh/penning49menu.html> (May 29, 2007).

5 | Ibid.

6 | Ibid.

7 | Ibid.

8 Larry Gara, Brenda E. Stevenson, and C. Peter Ripley, *Underground Railroad* (Washington, D.C.: National Park Service, 1990), p. 47.

9 Ibid., p. 52.

10 Bordewich, pp. 309–310.

11 John Hope Franklin and Loren Schweniger, *Runaway Slaves: Rebels on the Plantation* (New York: Oxford University Press, 1999), p. 163.

12 Bordewich, p. 110.

13 Ibid., pp. 111–112.

14 George Hendrick and Willene Hendrick, eds., *Fleeing for Freedom: Stories of the Underground Railroad As Told by Levi Coffin and William Still* (Chicago: Ivan R. Dee Publishers, 2004), p. 9.

15 Bordewich, p. 119.

16 Hendrick and Hendrick, p. 3.

CHAPTER 5. The Underground Railroad at Work

1 Fergus M. Bordewich, *Bound for Canaan: The Underground Railroad and the War for the Soul of America* (New York: Harper Collins, 2005), p. 323.

2 Ibid. p. 269.

3 David W. Blight, ed., *Passages to Freedom: The Underground Railroad in History and Memory* (Washington: Smithsonian Books, 2004), p. 112.

4 Larry Gara, Brenda E. Stevenson, and C. Peter Ripley, *Underground Railroad* (Washington, D.C.: National Park Service, 1990), p. 61.

5 George Hendrick and Willene Hendrick eds., *Fleeing for Freedom: Stories of the Underground*

Railroad As Told by Levi Coffin and William Still (Chicago: Ivan R. Dee Publishers, 2004), pp. 29–30.

6   John Hope Franklin and Afred A. Moss Jr., *From Slavery to Freedom: A History of African Americans* (New York: McGraw Hill, 1994), p. 185.

7   Hendrick and Hendrick, p. 43.

8   Ibid., p. 45.

9   Ibid., p. 79.

10   John P. Parker, *His Promised Land* (New York: W.W. Norton & Company, 1996), pp. 71–72.

11   Blight, p. 1.

CHAPTER 6. Black Workers on the Underground Railroad

1   Harriet Jacobs (writing under the name Linda Brent), *Incidents in the Life of a Slave Girl* (New York: The Modern Library, 2000), p. 168.

2   David W. Blight ed., *Passages to Freedom: The Underground Railroad in History and Memory* (Washington: Smithsonian Books, 2004), p. 99.

3   Ibid., p. 115.

4   Ibid., p. 114.

5   John Hope Franklin and Loren Schweniger, *Runaway Slaves: Rebels on the Plantation* (New York: Oxford University Press, 1999), p. 111.

6   Ibid.

7   Fergus M. Bordewich, *Bound for Canaan: The Underground Railroad and the War for the Soul of America* (New York: HarperCollins, 2005), p. 380.

Chapter Notes

8   The Peter Mott House and Museum, © 2007 <http://
www.petermotthouse.org/> (May 29, 2007).

9   Bordewich, p. 383.

10   Ibid., p. 410.

11   Ibid.

12   John P. Parker, *His Promised Land* (New York:
W.W. Norton & Company, 1996), pp. 100–101.

13   Ibid., p. 102.

14   Ibid., p. 103.

15   Ibid.

16   Frederick Douglass, *Narrative of the Life of
Frederick Douglass, an American Slave* (New York:
The Modern Library, 2000), p. 51.

17   Ibid., p. 63.

18   Ibid., pp. 74–75.

19   Ibid., p. 95.

20   Ibid.

21   John Hope Franklin and Afred A. Moss Jr., *From
Slavery to Freedom: A History of African
Americans* (New York: McGraw Hill, 1994), p. 214.

22   Douglass, p. 69.

CHAPTER 7. Harriet Tubman: The Moses of Her People

1   Leon Litwack and August Meier eds., *Black
Leaders of the Nineteenth Century* (Urbana:
University of Illinois Press, 1988), p. 48.

2   Catherine Clinton, *Harriet Tubman: The Road to
Freedom* (New York: Little, Brown and Company,
2004), p. 16.

3 Fergus M. Bordewich, *Bound for Canaan: The Underground Railroad and the War for the Soul of America* (New York: Harper Collins, 2005), p. 347.

4 Clinton, p. 10.

5 Bordewich, p. 347.

6 Clinton, p. 22.

7 Ibid., p. 38.

8 Bordewich, p. 349.

9 Ibid., p. 350.

10 Clinton, p. 44.

11 Bordewich, p. 350.

12 Ibid., p. 350.

13 Clinton, p. 83.

14 John Hope Franklin and Afred A. Moss Jr., *From Slavery to Freedom: A History of African Americans* (New York: McGraw Hill, 1994), p. 187.

15 Clinton, p. 91.

16 David W. Blight ed., *Passages to Freedom: The Underground Railroad in History and Memory* (Washington: Smithsonian Books, 2004), p. 201.

17 Clinton, p. 91.

18 Ibid., p. 87.

19 Litwack Meier, p. 47.

20 Blight, p. 207.

21 Ibid.

22 Clinton, p. 32.

Chapter 8. Free at Last!

1 Samuel Eliot Morison, *The Oxford History of the American People* (New York: Oxford University Press, 1965), p. 595.

Chapter Notes

2 William C. Davis, *Brother Against Brother* (Alexandria, Virginia: Time-Life Books, 1983), p. 109.

3 Aboard the Underground Railroad: A National Register Travel Itinerary, <http://www.cr.nps.gov/nr/travel/underground/> (April 4, 2007).

amendment—A change in a legal document.

annals—Documents or written history of a subject.

beacon—A light or bright shining object.

blights—Dirties or fouls a subject or thing.

bondage—The condition of slavery.

conspiracy—An agreement, usually secret, between several persons to carry out a plan or an action.

deemed—Judged or formed an opinion.

epilepsy—A disease characterized by a person fainting, having a seizure, or quickly falling into a deep sleep.

flog—To whip or beat a person.

hypocrite—A person who pretends to have a certain belief, even though he or she does not hold to or act upon that belief.

inherent—A truth or nature held within a person.

ironically—The use of words or actions that convey an opposite meaning.

moderation—Mild or reserved.

negro—Once used to refer to an African American, this term is now considered insulting.

nigger—An offensive, racist term used to refer to an African American.

noxious—Foul or offensive, as in a bad smell.

pander—To cater to the likes or dislikes of others.

portend—Something that serves as a warning or a threat of bad things to come.

ruse—A disguise or a false feature, like a mask, designed to conceal a true identity.

scourge—An instrument such as a whip used to hurt another person.

spontaneously—To do something immediately with little planning or thought.

trek—A long journey or hike.

veracity—Truthfulness.

Further Reading

Armentrout, David and Patricia. *The Emancipation Proclamation.* Vero Beach, Fla.: Rourke Publishing, 2005.

Collier, Christopher and James Lincoln. *Slavery and the Coming of the Civil War.* Tarrytown, N.Y.: Marshall Cavendish, 2000.

Collins, Kathleen. *Sojourner Truth: Equal Rights Advocate.* New York: Rosen Publishing, 2004.

Fleming, Alice. *Frederick Douglass: From Slave to Statesman.* New York: Rosen Publishing, 2004.

Haskins, J. and K. Benson. *Following Freedom's Star: The Story of the Underground Railroad.* Tarrytown, N.Y.: Marshall Cavendish, 2000.

January, Brendan. *John Brown's Raid on Harpers Ferry.* Danbury, Conn.: Childrens Press, 2000.

Landau, Elaine. *Slave Narratives: The Journey to Freedom.* Danbury, Conn.: Childrens Press, 2000.

Lester, Julius. *To Be A Slave.* New York: Dial Books, 1998.

Shone, Rob and Anita Ganeri. *Harriet Tubman: The Life of an African-American Abolitionist.* New York: Rosen Publishing, 2005.

Internet Addresses

**National Underground Railroad
Freedom Center**

**National Underground Railroad Network
to Freedom**
<www.cr.nps.gov/ugrr/>

**New York History Net—The Harriet
Tubman Home**
<www.nyhistory.com/harriettubman/>

Index

Index